Creative
Reboot

BIS Publishers
Borneostraat 80-A
1094 CP Amsterdam
The Netherlands
T +31 (0)20 515 02 30
bis@bispublishers.com
www.bispublishers.com

ISBN 978 90 6369 632 0

BIS PUBLISHERS

CREATIVE REBOOT

CATALYSING CREATIVE INTELLIGENCE

**Barbara Doran, Rodger Watson,
Diana Vo & Others**

contents
page

o6   Using this book:
introduction

08   Framing and
pragmatic creativity

creativity, play and flow

14   Who can be creative?

17   Play is serious

18   Play histories

20   Types of play

24   Flow

26   Self regulation

28   Sensing

31   Journaling and reflection

32   Case study

probing and blitzing

36   30 circles

38   Metaphor catching

40   Renku

42   Think inside the box

44   Why? Why? Why? Why? Why?

46   Design a more beautiful question

48   Ignorance Mapping

50   Layers on Layers

52   Case study

visualising

 # conversations

56	Visual stretch
58	Symbols
60	Sketching
62	Rich pictures
64	Exquisite corpse
66	Movement mapping
68	Gestalt
72	Portrait
74	Case study

100	Small talk
102	Social spaces
104	Gesture and mimicry
106	Material talk
108	Marking and yarning
110	Audio describing
112	Creative alt text
114	Conversation cafe
116	Case study

 # scaling

 # stories

78	Scale and simple rules
80	Replicating patterns
82	Back cast and future cast
84	Motion
86	Binary Messages
88	Eames power of 10
90	Create an album of music
94	Memory board
96	Case study

120	Create a character
122	Scenography as story
124	Voicing
126	Rituals
128	Animate
130	Memory palace
132	Make a story
134	Collage
136	Case study
138	Case study

140	Contributors

Using this book: introduction

Creative Reboot comes as a kit. The book has been designed to carry around so you can practice creativity easily and in different settings. It also comes with exercise cards that can be quick, shareable and gamified. Together the cards and kit work in two ways – to build creative skills and to stimulate ongoing creative deftness. The book provides a sequential path that helps imaginative diverging (expanding) and converging (bringing together) through guided creative exercises that can be done individually and collaboratively. Once you become familiar with the cycle, you can take the process of creativity further by choosing different combinations or by gamifying the cards to cross-pollinate and push the boundaries of possibility.

There are six chapters in this book each working into a frame that is supported by primer and extender exercises, and illustrated in seven case studies profiling pioneers of this emergent practice. Grounded in a cross-section of scholarly and applied understanding, each exercise is supported by a deeper seedbed of underpinning influences and pointers to more granular and embodied ways of noticing. The first chapter, 'Creativity, play and flow' explores foundational qualities linked to creativity along with useful approaches that help sustain a creative mindset. The following five chapters take you through a journey that helps free up allegiances to habitual ways of thinking that are inhibiting. The exercises in 'Probing and Blitzing' and 'Visualising' widen ways of perceiving while 'Scaling' invites relationships between bigger vision perspectives and action on the ground.

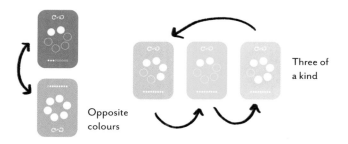

Three of a kind

Opposite colours

With new quests of the possible on the table, 'Conversations' opens up what it means to connect and 'Stories' harnesses the rich palette we use in mobilising practical action and meaning. Cumulatively, the exercises illuminate new through lines beyond the frameworks that we might be blinded by or bound to even though they no longer serve us. Whether you are an analytical thinker or an accomplished creative professional, perceptual shape shifting transforms as we travel deeper and wider.

To extend this kit you can combine and recombine the exercises looking for adjacent possibilities, serendipitous associations and unseen connections. Use the card numbering and colour systems like dominoes and playing cards. Play with pairs, three of a kind or a run in numbers. Match cards by colour- e.g. similar tones of dark and light or opposing colours such as yellow and purple. Make your own rules and bend them. Playing in this way generates creative fitness, helps ideas cross pollinate and reveals paths for changing our minds. Each section of the book is supported by case studies that have done exactly this – created new ways into the world.

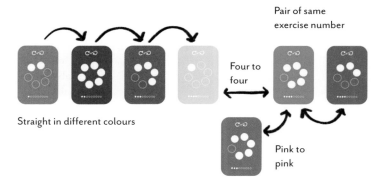

Pair of same exercise number

Four to four

Straight in different colours

Pink to pink

Framing and pragmatic creativity

If what you have been doing isn't working, try something else.

Issues are framed in certain ways. The framing is either deliberate or emerges over time. Either way, the framing is true and not true. We'll use the framing a real case study, framed as a *health* issue as an example.

Framing something as a *health* issue can send us down a very different path to if we frame the same thing as a *wellbeing* issue.

Tony fell from a ladder in his bicycle shop and sustained a spinal injury. Tony received expert medical treatment and over three months made a full physical recovery. The time away from work was very hard. The day-to-day connections that Tony had with his colleagues and customers were lost in this time, and he really missed them. Tony became depressed and anxious about leaving his home.

The frames we create become part of our societal narrative, we become expert in navigating them. Whole disciplines emerge within these frames.

From a *health* frame, we see *Medicine* as the dominant discipline area which encompasses Medical Physicians, Nurses, Radiography, Chemists, etc. All of these practitioners are highly educated in the **rules** of their frame. In practice they draw on these **rules** and their professional experience to determine the 'correct' action to take. All of these actions then contribute to achieving the *health* **outcome.**

Drawing on the American Pragmatist Philosopher, Charles Sanders Peirce we can unpack this through logic;

The pre-determined **outcome,** "health" is reached through the pre-determined **rules** "medicine" which through drawing on experience we determine what **actions** or "treatment" is appropriate.

Peirce rereferred to this way of thinking as *explanatory abduction*. This is a useful, valuable, and productive way of thinking. But it isn't all that is possible when using abductive thinking.

The American philosopher of science, Thomas S. Kuhn, in his 1962 book 'The Structure of Scientific Revolutions' spoke of paradigms. Within a paradigm the vast majority of thinking happens within the conceptual boundaries of 'known' *outcome*, 'pre-determined' *rule* and inferred action. Through this logic an *evidence base* is established by testing and evaluating the efficacy of the treatments. But what if we need a different way of looking at things? What if the *health, medicine, treatment* formula isn't getting us the results we truly desire? Peirce would put forward a different type of logic; *innovative abduction.*

Innovative abduction could be a heavy term if we dwelled on it, but dwelling is never the way of the Pragmatist. In our practice, *innovative abduction* is a playful space. We draw on both Kuhn and Peirce through the work of Kees Dorst and his 2015 book 'Frame Innovation: Create new thinking by design'. The practice we developed, 'Designing for the common good' makes space for playful, creative exploration. We playfully frame, de-frame, and re-frame. We suspend the *Rule* and *Outcome* variables and draw on playful and creative ways of exploring the deeper questions of meaning.

It is just here, in this conceptual space that we create some time and space to escape analysis paralysis.

Tony received an unusual prescription from his regular Doctor. Instead of the pain killers that had usually been part of the routine Doctor visits, Tony was given a 12-week prescription to join a local Life Drawing class.

By *re-framing* the situation from an **outcome** of *health* to an **outcome** of *wellbeing* the underlying issue of isolation is broached. This real-world case study is an example of *innovative abduction*. It is also an example of how *innovative abduction* can then fit neatly back into the paradigm. Not so radical that it will disrupt a whole way of working, but radical enough to have created a new addition to the accepted *rules*.

The thinking required is not rocket science. It requires disciplined thought to suspend what we already know, or assume, in order to allow for the emergence of new frames that can then be tested.

creativity,
play

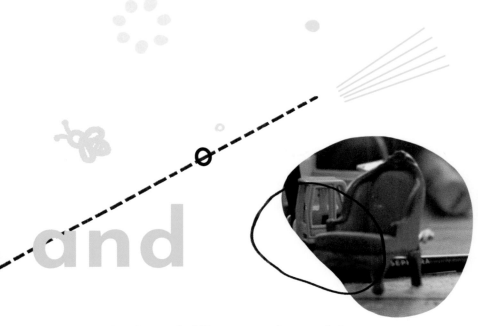

and

How often do you play? Do you notice how people have different ways of playing?

When you give yourself space to be creative you build fitness, and with that comes confidence. Like most skills in life, creativity responds to practice and in doing so, we become more aware of our unique strengths, the weaknesses we can improve upon and those that benefit most from collaborating with others.

In honing our personal and collective creativity, we open up the landscape of imagination and innovation.

Everyone has a different creative journey. Before we dig into how we can be more creative, we first need to examine some of our current assumptions about creativity.

flow

What if I'm not creative?

Maybe you don't see the work you currently do as creative, or feel you don't have that 'creative' spark in you. If this is you, know this – you are in fact capable of creativity! Though the myth that some people are creative and others are analytical is still pervasive in society, the truth is that creativity is not simply a matter of inherent ability. For artists, engineers, philosophers, scientists, and all other types of creatives, their skill is developed through sustained practice.

Throughout this kit you will be introduced to strategies for building creative habits and getting that practice in.

Divergent thinking

Let's try flexing our creative muscles! In one minute, how many uses can you think of for this cardboard box? Time yourself and start writing!

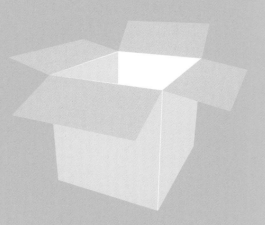

Where to from here?

As you navigate this kit you will trial a range of creative exercises drawn from a cross section of disciplines. Some exercises will feel easier to connect with than others, this is part of the creative journey. Ideally, you will find creative companions to discuss your experiences and make plans to keep exploring.

There is one thing that numerous studies on creativity have found and that is creativity does best when we are in an open, relaxed state. It's a state where we ask our critical judge to hold off, where we suspend our utility focus. It's a state that involves asking ourselves 'what's the purpose of this' commentator, so we let ourselves into a curious and playful place where new ways of seeing, noticing and doing can arise. It's also where we can revisit assumptions about our aptitudes and look at the way we work with others. Stepping into an open mode of inquiry is the starting point. Just like all habits, practice and repetition transfers short term pulses into long term patterns.

Creativity involves making new kinds of connections. It isn't exclusive to a medium, practice or discipline. It can happen anywhere, anytime and often brings together unlikely or unseen relationships. This is why an open minded space is foundational. We won't find new ways of seeing without releasing the hold of fixed patterns of perception. The arts are often linked to creativity and while they are not the exclusive domain there are tips and practices that can help foster creative fitness.

The open mode, is a relaxed, expansive, and less purposeful mode in which we're probably more contemplative, more inclined to humor (which always accompanies a wider perspective), and, consequently, more playful.

It's a mood in which curiosity for its own sake can operate because we're not under pressure to get a specific thing done quickly. We can play, and that is what allows our natural creativity to surface.

— John Cleese

Play is serious

So far we've learnt that your creative muscles can be toned through training just like your physical muscles.

Let's extend the fitness analogy a little further. Getting fit isn't just about going outside and doing as much exercise as you can straight away. You need to stretch, you may need particular equipment or routines, and you need to combine your exercise with a balanced diet. So too, with creativity, you should begin by considering how you can create an environment that sustains creativity. Part of this is developing a sense for when the time is right for 'open' mode/playful activity - it can be as simple as the times during coffee breaks, passing someone in the corridor, to cooking and folding washing.

The comedy sketches of writer and actor John Cleese are among some of the most well known in the world. In one of his many lectures on creativity, Cleese explains how his creative work is unlocked through play, which is only achieved by claiming a space for play and setting it in contrast to ordinary life.

Creating a space for play isn't just about rearranging the furniture so there's room to jump around. It's about moving into a mindset that isn't constrained by the parameters of everyday time and space. Cleese refers to this mindset as 'open' mode, and describes it as a relaxed and playful space where curiosity can operate for its own sake rather than be utility driven.

Part of creating a space for play involves figuring out when and where we are most likely to slip into this 'open' mode. One unexpected place to look is to nature – primates, birds and many mammals have been observed in this playful creative mode.

Scan the QR code to hear John Cleese's talk on creativity and the 'open' mode.

Play histories

As you begin to think about how to cultivate your sense of play, it's helpful to reflect on a time when play probably came naturally to you.

Play is intrinsically linked to learning. As children we set up and are drawn into play scenarios where open inquiry and self regulation are explored. Children are great improvisers and adept in harnessing whatever is around into play settings. Whether it's cardboard boxes turned into cubby houses, Lego, blocks, sandpits, rough and tumble play...the list goes on.

Through play we begin to tune into the way we like to learn and how to work with or alongside others. Play is the optimal state for developing our open, receptive states and the bonus is that we learn at the same time.

Scan the QR code to hear Dr Stuart Brown, a psychiatrist and leading researcher into the psychology of play, share his understanding of play.

Play behavior is one of the most important parts of being human and it supports life long learning. In seeking to become a creative caretaker, look to support situations and environments that evoke glee and spontaneity.

What can you do now to recreate playful feelings?

Reflecting on our history with play helps us:

- To identify where we have experienced meaning and fun (flow) in our own lives
- Empathise with how others might be motivated
- Design engaging games
- Experiment and learn through feedback
- Learn to engage with open curiosity
- Figure out ways to collaborate with other who might play differently

The question prompts on the page will help remind you of things you might have forgotten. Play histories create mental pictures of your attitudes and the emotions they are connected to. Reject any judgemental or sceptical thoughts that try to interrupt this reflection.

What did you do as a child that got you really excited?

Are there visual images that come to mind?

How did you feel?

Were you alone or with other people?

Types of play

Our play histories indicate where and how we have played in our past. They also offer insight into the roles we adopt alone and with others as we learn. We can often recognise these roles in our adult lives not only in our work choices but also in group settings. There are numerous psychometric tests that look for traits, aptitudes and orientations. They can be helpful as long as they don't confine us with labels that put us in a box. There's plenty of evidence that we are neuroplastic too.

Dr Stuart Brown identified 8 types of player personalities. These personalities are useful in helping us to find the part of ourselves that steps into open mode. Equally so, it helps us to appreciate the diverse ways others play and how there are symbiotic relationships when we play together.

Each of us has a dominant play mode. This play mode can morph and change as context changes and as we age and grow, but in essence, it is the basis of how we are naturally drawn to interact with the world through play. Take a moment to read the descriptions of each player personality on the following pages, and consider how closely you connect with each description.

There are also times where we may switch roles depending on the context. For instance there is mutability in the role of storyteller, director and artist or competitor, director and kinesthete. There is skill in reading the context and noticing play in motion.

The Joker

Jokers love nonsense, silly sounds, being foolish and lightening the mood. They frequently connect with others through their jokes and love to make others laugh.

The Kinesthete

Kinesthetes love to engage in physical movement. Although they enjoy physical games, competition is not required; it is more about the movement. Play can range from clearing land to playing football, cooking and sewing.

The Explorer

Explorers relish novel challenges. Whether visiting new places, researching new subjects or under-going journeys where awareness is developed or deepened. Exploration is a tool for provoking imagination and remaining creative.

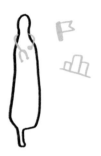

The Competitor

Competitors love specific rules and goals. They want to know how to win and who won – whether team sports or solo endeavours, physical or mental. They love scorekeeping and keeping track of progress.

The Director

Directors enjoy planning and executing. They frequently take the lead in teams, organise social occasions and coordinate events such as performances, festivals, parties and group gatherings.

The Collector

Collectors love to hunt for and gather objects: the best, the most interesting and unusual. They might also collect experiences, like visiting countries or seeing every show of a touring band. Collectors can play alone or as part of a social team or club. They also enjoy categorising.

The Artist/Creator

The Artist/Creator loves to make things. They transform spaces into rooms with atmosphere and possibility. They often reside in workshops and studios overflowing with treasures and supplies. Some Artists/Creators like to make something brand new from a blank canvas, while others like to take things apart or reassemble. Regardless of whether they are recognised for their talents, the true Artist/Creator simply loves the process.

The Storyteller

Storytellers can make themselves part of any story. They take joy not only in telling stories but also in listening. They might relish in reading books, watching movies and making versions of their own. They love metaphor and symbolism and use them to make sense of the world. Storytellers are unique in that they can bring play to almost any activity or event.

Flow

As we've seen, play is not simply frivolous or aimless – it is a channel for achieving an optimal state of openness and receptivity. This state can be understood as something more than joy, or focused attention: it is a state of flow.

20th century psychologist Mihaly Csikszentmihalyi first coined the term 'flow' to describe a mental state of heightened focus, pleasure and immersion in an activity. Csikszentmihalyi interviewed experts in various fields: artists, scientists, politicians, business leaders and athletes. All described a state of focus and pleasure when the task they were doing matched their skills: not too challenging as to be impossible, but not too easy as to be trivial and boring.

Research has shown associations between flow states and decreased activity in the prefrontal cortex. Inhibition of the prefrontal lobe may enable the implicit mind to take over, allowing more brain areas to communicate freely and engage in a creative process.

Flow matrix diagram

The flow matrix diagram is a tool to help you assess your flow state when involved in creative activities. It providesa useful framework to revisit as you reflect on the new creative methods and practices you try.

CSIKSZENTMIHALYI DESCRIBES EIGHT CHARACTERISTICS OF FLOW:

1. COMPLETE CONCENTRATION ON THE TASK

FOCUS

2. CLARITY OF GOALS AND REWARD IN MIND AND IMMEDIATE FEEDBACK

3. TRANSPORTATION OF TIME (SPEEDING UP/SLOWING DOWN)

FREEDOM

4. THE EXPERIENCE IS INTRINSICALLY REWARDING

5. EFFORTLESSNESS AND EASE

6. THERE IS A BALANCE BETWEEN CHALLENGE AND SKILLS

FEEDBACK

7. ACTIONS AND AWARENESS ARE MERGED, LOSING SELF-CONSCIOUS RUMINATION

INCREMENTAL CHALLENGE

8. THERE IS A FEELING OF CONTROL OVER THE TASK

Self regulation

Self-regulation is the ability to manage the bio-feedback linked to emotions and reactions in service of your longer term goals. Practicing self-regulation involves staying calm when you find yourself in an upsetting or frustrating situation, and responding quickly and positively to change.

Psychologists, educators and health practitioners each work with the dynamics of self regulation but it's not often framed as a creative practice. In fact, it is – learning to navigate creativity can be a lifelong vocation that is like an ongoing balancing act. It simultaneously requires a kind of still attention and a willingness to move. There are cycles of growth and energy countered by steadfastness amidst a sense of stasis.

Developing a creative practice is rarely a straightforward, linear process. It may take some time to find the approaches that will work for you. Having the ability to self-regulate will mean you are able to embrace uncertainty as a natural part of development while honing an awareness that is attuned to interoception (inner sensing) and exteroception (sensing outer conditions). Together these skills are often dubbed intuition or an attuned sixth sense.

There are many strategies that support self-regulation such as cognitive reframing, tuning into your senses and engaging in meditative activities like taking a walk in nature or having a shower. Part of your creative reboot journey will involve learning what works for you.

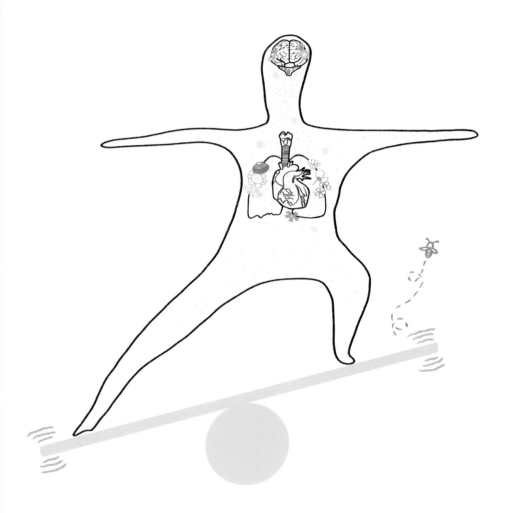

Sensing

"Western Culture has long separated the mind from the body; the brain has been privileged as the source of intellect, with the rest of the body annexed as mere matter. But the new field of 'embodied cognition', offers a richer, more holistic view of intelligence that involves the whole body."
Guy Claxton, author of 'Intelligence in the Flesh'.

As advances in technologies have enabled mapping and tracking of our neural circuits, a new view of the mind has developed. The brain is no longer considered to be housed in our skulls alone. In his book 'Mindsight' psychiatrist Dan Siegal show how a cross-disciplinary group of researchers and philosophers interested in the mind settled on a shared definition that "the human mind is a relational and embodied process that regulates flows of energy and information".

To augment this view, research from the field of embodied psychology has clearly demonstrated that qualities such as colour, light, texture and temperature can significantly influence how we filter the world even though we might rationally deny it. Thalma Lobel has distilled this research in her book 'Sensation. The New Science of Physical Intelligence'. The book explores fascinating studies that reveal how embodied information such as how texture and temperature influence our evaluations of the warmth or trustability of people and situations.

We can look to this renewed understanding of our body mind by tapping into our senses to harness new creative possibilities. Opening ourselves up to our sensory experience can simultaneously enhance self regulation and activate unexplored neural connections that can generate new ideas or help us see our stubborn problems in a new light.

Warm up your senses

A good way to warm up a creativity and prime a flow states to invite your senses in by taking them on a date. We often don't give much time to considering how our senses contribute to our experiences, yet we know they can significantly influence our perceptions.

For this task go on a date with each sense for an hour. You may wish to focus on a shared space, a smaller room or the whole environment.

SOUND

"In an acoustic environ we are always at the center".
Yi-Fu Tuan, acoustic artist

Our world is a rich, subtle assemblage of sounds that provide us with a 3D sense of place. Unlike other senses, our ears are always open. Listening is an act of finding our place in the world, primes us for action, helps invoke images and memories while expanding our spatial awareness. Sound also influences our moods (e.g. curiosity, frustration, anxiety, fear, boredom, and tranquility) though, what may be music to one may be noise to another.

Note the sounds:
- That give your environment personality
- Prime people to take actions
- Prompt memories
- Irritate or stimulatescreate a feeling of space/3D

In your notations note the shape of the sounds. Were they:
- Louder and quieter
- Higher and lower
- Longer and shorter
- Irregular and periodical

TOUCH

Our skin is our biggest organ. It provides us with data on texture, pressure, temperature and movement. Not only that, our skins give off electro conductive signals that show we know something before our conscious brains do. Hold a warm drink for someone on a cold day and you will think they are a kinder, more generous and trust-worthy person. Thick paper CV's are related to 'weight' of skills while hard textures (think your seat or footpaths) are equated with difficulty.

Spend an hour evaluating the touch of your environment. Notice:
- Textures and your associations (clothes, surfaces, materials you handle)
- Temperatures
- What, how and who you touch
- How others respond to tactile information

SIGHT

Sight is often regarded as the king of the senses but we rarely stop to consider how we see. Sight involves moving our heads and eyes which, draws together information from our right and left visual fields. Sight involves, responding to contrasts in texture, patterns of light and dark and noticing landmarks.

Go on a date with a colour per hour. Date 5 colours. Pick a colour (any colour) and look for its presence. Record the frequency, object/item and emotional timbre.
A note on colour and emotion:
Some colours are culturally mediated but red is the only one found to elicit universal responses.
Did you know Red affects:
- Physical performance, verbal and mathematical performance
- Responses linked to danger and anxiety
- Sexual behavior

TASTE AND SMELL (OLFACTION)

Though these senses have different pathways, we often experience them together partly because they have a direct line into the parts of our brain where non-verbal memory and emotion are housed. Both smell and taste can radically influence our reactions, associations and once fused in memory are difficult to untangle.

Note the smells in your environment.
- What associations or memories do they stimulate?
- Do they give you clues about materials, chemicals and aging processes?
- Do some smells trigger hunger or desire to eat?
- What are the kinds of food and drink smells?

Journaling and reflection

Journaling is a helpful tool for personal creative practice. It can help us express ourselves, process and uncover ideas and think creatively. It also allows us to observe and respond to the surrounding environment.

Creative professionals frequently use journaling as a tool for supporting creativity by using methods and practices drawn from various disciplines encompassing the arts, design, science and other modes that help listening, noticing and recording. Journaling also involves a process of experimenting and adapting to fit your own professional and personal life. Documenting the results and reflections can lead to new methodologies and ideas.

There are many ways to explore journalling from analogue to digital tools. Testing various methods can be a way to find what's right for you. Using materials and tools that best suit your process is important, although it may take some time to work out what's right for you. A variety of tools from a paper diary, digital apps, paint, pens or pencils can be used. Collecting snippets from daily life such as photos, receipts, tickets, pressed leaves and flowers can also add layers of memory and texture.

Justine Hauser – Unlocking the written word.

Justine serves in the defence force and is accustomed to working in highly structured environments. In her profession, actions become like muscle memory. The actions all hang together in a broader process that achieves the tactical objectives of her team, her unit, and the broader defence force. Each action must be done right. It can be a life and death environment where precision is key.

As a parent Justine has been navigating a complex situation with her 6-year-old son G. G had fallen behind his peer group at school. He undertook a benchmarking test at the beginning of the year and scored 9%. He had become disengaged and had lost his curiosity. The test score helped the system jump into action. G took a number of medical tests and the helped explain why he was struggling to engage with school activities.

"G's ear drum is not moving to sound, he can hear but; it is like hearing under water and certain sounds are not heard correctly, mainly sh, ch, ish, ff sounds.

He is also unable to track with his eyes without moving his head, this means that he physically exhausted by mid-morning after attempting his tasks."

G was given glasses to help reduce the exhaustion, and Justine began working with him to reengage with his schoolwork. Justine drew on a Masters subject that she was doing; Creative Practices & Methods.

"The first step was creating flow and play. I liked the idea of John Cleese's 'space for play' that will allow the 'open' mode mindset. I used toilet humour and gave Gabriel coloured pencils and asked him to draw the toilet and what we might find in the toilet. It was hilarious and it got him to use pencils and draw. He also started telling me stories about how things end up in the toilet.

I think when that happened we reached that space for play and an open mindset. Each week we came up a new environment and what we may find in it."

Justine used six types of exercises in engaging with G:

·   Embracing creativity and playfulness
·   Probing – the art of exploring
·   Visualising – tapping into the senses and how we communicate
·   Scale – traveling with time, space and materials
·   Conversations – becoming fluent with the obvious and not so obvious
·   Stories – the biology and magic of making sense together

In the last week of the school term G scored 89% in the same benchmark test.

"I am not sure which interventions were the main driver of the dramatic change, but I would like to think that they all contributed – like vitamins in a system they have given G the health holistically to unlocking the written word. All the teachers had noticed a dramatic change not just in his ability in reading and writing but in other areas, art and even sport. Also his willingness to participate and engage has increased as his confidence has grown. His curiosity is back, and we now have new tools to explore the world with."

probing

and

To come up with novel and expanded ideas we need to think fast and slow. The probing and blitzing exercises in this chapter help us with both.

Probing is a way of playing with assumptions and looking for deeper insights into the patterns we live with, revealing our values and implicit or unspoken rules for action. Probing is a way to see beyond the surface – it asks us to find questions, ask more of what we know, how we know, seek out what we don't know and into the abyss of what we don't know we don't know!

Blitzing involves fast thinking and accessing our tacit knowledge, the stuff our bodies know ahead of our consciousness. Getting to work, eating dinner, having a shower: all are goal-oriented, mostly automatic tasks with a reflexive set of actions linked to them. Our default responses are fast neurochemical circuits that take the path of least resistance. Without challenge, these responses chug along, filtering out other possibilities. This isn't bad, but when we are looking for a new angle there are things we can do to dive deeper into the repositories of our experience and dig up a treasure trove of possibilities.

With a new and expanded menu of options on the table, we can ponder, trial new arrangements and observe how they digest.

30 circles

Background

The 30 circles exercise is an oldie but a goodie that gets pulled out in most design thinking workshops or when designers are wanting to ignite their creativity. Traced back to Bob McKim of the Stanford Design Program, it is simple and quick to do. It's a great warm up that helps ideas flow and asks the self-censor to step to the back while highlighting how speed and quantity of ideas partner well with adaptive imagination.

The great thing about 30 circles is it can be used iteratively – do one cycle, reflect on insights and then do it again. It is also a good tool for bringing creative minds together.

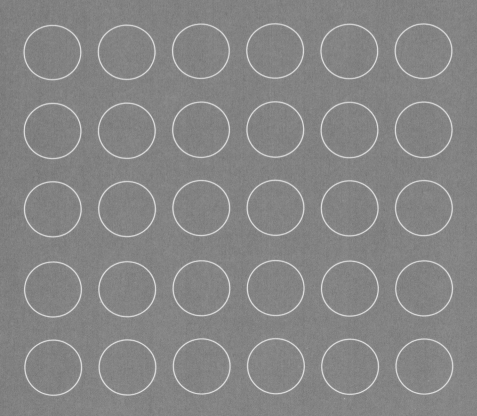

Try it yourself

This exercise works best individually or in pairs.
Get something to draw with and a piece of paper with 30 blank circles on it of approximately the same size. You can draw the circles yourself on an A4/A3 page or print out a template on the book website.

Set a three minute timer. Try and turn as many of the blank circles as possible into recognisable objects before the timer goes off. This is not about the quality of drawing, it's about how many ideas you can come up with.

As you look at the results, notice:
- How many circles did you use – 10, 15, 20? (Most people don't finish)
- Next, look for diversity or flexibility in ideas
- Are the ideas derived from the circular shape?
- Did you combine two or more (a bike or a traffic light)?
- Were the rules clear? Did you assume the rules were more strict?
- What are your favourite ideas?
- Push two ideas together - do you get a new idea? Can you make a headline or title?
- What feelings arose? Did your inner censor speak up?

If in a pair, use these prompts to compare your responses with your partner.

X

time is ticking . . .

~~evil and bitter person!~~

x

bright future

Background

Metaphors are powerful short cuts to personal and collective ways of making sense of the world. Metaphors often embody cues to how we bind physical and emotional associations with shared cultural values.

Cognitive linguist George Lakoff claims that many metaphors innate to our understanding of the world are the result of deep neurological connections formed in childhood, such as the association between warmth and kindness or the notion that up means more. In this way, Lakoff suggests that we are always thinking in metaphor.

Metaphors make use of contrasting associations: warm/cold, soft/hard, day/night. Contrasts help us create distinctions and they can form the basis of how we order and prioritise especially if we place them into fixed binary relationships. Equally so, they can reveal unquestioned biases and opportunities to reimagine things. Many metaphors are also based in sensory experiences, and can contain hidden associations between senses and thoughts that often go unnoticed. Take a look at the sensory metaphor cloud we've developed, and feel free to add your own!

slow decline

bittersweet

quiet as a mouse.

jampacked

sharp increase ___

Try it yourself

Over the course of a week, notice the metaphors in your world. They are in conversations, emails, signage, lyrics, advertising, t-shirts – everywhere! Jot them down.

Use the metaphors you have found or if needed search for more online. Scan through and find a few that connect. Make notes:
- What are the key words - what are the physical and emotional associations?
- Are there implied hierarchies?
- Are there contrasts or binaries?

Now spend some time playing with the metaphors:
- Try to change their meaning!
- Can you turn a mechanical process or a living process?
- Replace or invert words and sensations – what happens?

What do you identify about power, hierarchy, assumptions? Find something you'd like to change in your world and make a metaphor that fits.

 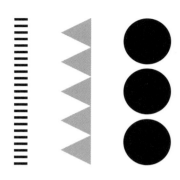

Background

Renku or haikai-no-renga is a long established Japanese art form – the art of collaborative poetry and metaphor creation.

This exercise in collective creativity and trust must be done with others – at least three, though possible with large groups too. This is a hybrid Renku taster where creative collaboration follows a few simple rules to guiding form, rhythm and theme. This sets up a space somewhere between a game with boundaries and the open exploration of play. In the midst, it is a joy to see the poetic images that arise like a colourful chemical reaction. Trust the rules and let your instinct rise. You can jiggle the words but don't overthink it.

At the end look for lines or verses that elude or directly link to metaphors. Are there new ideas or frames that appear?

 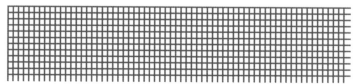

Try it yourself

Try making your own Renku with others. There are many different forms of Renku, but here's one method to get you started:

THEME - PLAY
SUB-THEME - CREATIVITY

Rules
Take turns for each line
Follow the theme and structure guide

Ist verse	2nd verse	3rd verse	4th verse	Share
Theme:	*Theme:*	*Theme:*	*Theme:*	*Read aloud*
Play – explicit	*Play – explicit*	*Creativity – explicit*	*Play and Creativity – indirect*	*to group*
				What are your reflections?
Structure:	*Structure:*	*Structure:*	*Structure:*	
3 lines	*2 lines*	*3 lines*	*2 lines*	*How did you feel doing this?*
line I 3 syllables	line I 3 syllables	line I 3 syllables	line I 3 syllables	
line 2 5 syllables	line 2 5 syllables	line 2 5 syllables	line 2 5 syllables	
line 3 4 syllables		line 3 4 syllables		

Background

Creativity is often linked to thinking outside the box but often constraints and focused attention on the internal elements of a situation can be revealing and stimulate new insights. Many creatives describe how limitations can actually help reimagine how resources are used and reframe situations that have gotten stuck in habitual ways of thinking.

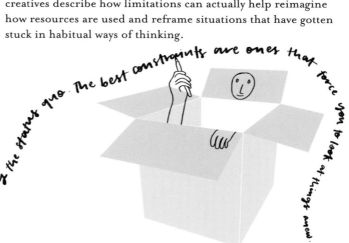

Creative constraints don't need to be constraints imposed by the status quo. The best constraints are ones that force you to look at things anew.

Invert
Flip the assumption. For example: restaurants normally provide customers with a menu when they arrive, but what if a restaurant only provided customers a menu when they leave?

Deny
Reject the assumption. For example: usually customers pay for food and service. What if customers were not charged for food and service?

Scale
Expand the assumption. For example: Restaurants offer three course meals, but what about a restaurant offering a 30 course meal?

Try it yourself

Pick something from your environment. It can be anything, don't worry if it seems random. For example:

- Stuff on your desk/work station
- Charts, graphs and print outs
- Receipts and tickets
- Formulas and recipes
- Clothing and shoes
- Washing and hygiene
- Coffee cups/wrappers/plates

- Signs and directions
- Building features
- Artwork/posters/advertising
- Transport
- Music or media
- Plants

Do one of the following actions and watch for what happens. Note down any questions this exercise provokes.

- Take out a part: What happens? What would you do? What would others do? Would the system work the same way? Are there easy replacements? What could you do to make the object function in a different way?
- Interrupt its function or how it is used: What if it was broken, didn't work, couldn't be accessed? What if it was combined with other objects in your environment?
- Deny its use or place: What if you can't use it, access it or it was absent?
- Make small shifts – put it in the wrong place: Invert it or put in its place something that is an opposition, e.g. upside down, outside, inside, valuable, invaluable.

Background

The 5 Whys is a simple method that can lead to developing beautiful questions. Japanese inventor and founder of Toyota - Sakichi Toyoda developed the 5 Whys technique in the 1930s and its popularity has since spread across the globe. The art of questioning can be linked to many practices including philosophy, science, motivational psychology, business and organisational decisions. There are also links to Socractic questioning and the practices of empirical reasoning. These techniques can lead us to underlying motivations and sets of associations – to the 'what if's' and 'how might's'.

Asking questions of your reasoning and assumptions is an impactful way of interrogating the underlying archeology or logic of cause and effect. The 5 Whys, when thoughtfully applied is a simple method that involves asking 'why' something is so, in answering a new question emerges. By repeating this sequence of question and answer, continued probing creates a pathway to the underlying assumptions, associations, actions and/or decisions that draw themes to the surface. You can see this process in the nested diagram below.

Try it yourself

Think of a problem space or challenge you're experiencing and jot down a bunch of questions that surround the issue.

For each question, probe by asking why and then ask why of your response. Continue on for 5 rounds but if you think there's further to go, continue until you feel like you're landing into a space that resonates deeply.

On your way look out for concepts or dynamics that might be framing the issue/s. Are there myths, metaphors, values, disciplinary biases, historical influences, hidden assumptions or specific exclusions?

When you've responded to your questions by probing, see if you can identify clusters or adjacent influences. Did you find through lines from unexpected fields?

See if you can arrive at a new question that anchors or reframes your challenge.

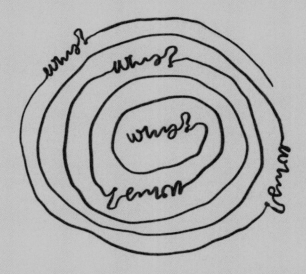

Background

Having questions is an innate human trait. As children, we grow up questioning everything as a way of learning how the world works. Unfortunately, the traditional education system most people go through discourages people from asking the 'wrong' kinds of questions, ultimately leading to people asking fewer questions in life than they should!

Asking beautiful questions to lead you further into your field of inquiry and search for connections is part of the heartland of creativity. Thinking about questions this way gets us thinking beyond the surface level of a situation and links deeper reflection to the bigger picture.

In his book 'A More Beautiful Question', Warren Berger cites the revelatory questions that inspired a number of successful innovations:

What if we could map the DNA of music? - Pandora

Why can't everyone accept credit cards? - Square

Why aren't football players urinating more? - Gatorade

Try it yourself

Design a question to sit with and explore.

It can be helpful to limit your question to an environment, time frame or situations like:
· In the context of….
· How might
· What if…..

Throughout the week, note the perspective shifts that occur while contemplating these questions.

"A beautiful question is an ambitious yet actionable question that can begin to shift the way we perceive or think about something – and that might serve as a catalyst to bring about change." – Warren Berger

Background

The ignorance map was developed by researcher Ann Kerwin while Philosopher-in-Residence of the Curriculum on Medical Ignorance at the University of Arizona Medical School. Ignorance mapping aims to help you interrogate your knowledge, and assumptions about your knowledge: the Known Unknowns, Unknown Unknowns, Unknown Knowns and all in between.

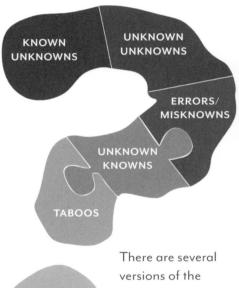

There are several versions of the ignorance map, but the one we'll use contains the sections described.

Known Unknowns
Everything you know you don't know. These could include adjacent possibilities ('I know X but would like to know Y') or future scenarios ('Yesterday I did X, tomorrow I could do Y').

Unknown Unknowns
Everything you don't know you don't know. To explore these, ask yourself:
· If we'd known…
· We could never have known…
· What if…

Errors/Misknowns
Everything you think you know, but don't. One way to approach these is through writing down your assumptions and then challenging or reversing them.

Unknown Knowns
Everything you don't know you know. What's your gut instinct, your least 'engineered' response?

Taboos
Dangerous, polluting or forbidden knowledge. What is the most dangerous 'discovery' you could articulate? Who would be endangered and why?

Denials
All the things that are too painful to know, so you don't. Is there some knowledge that you really don't want to confront about yourself when tackling this challenge?

Try it yourself

Reflect on the zeitgeist – the sociocultural environment around you. What comes up for you might be influenced by the place you work, your habitat, social networks and the media you consume.

Jot down a few themes that seem persistent. Choose the one that invokes tension, paradox and emotional charge.

Write responses to the theme using the ignorance map prompts.
Imagine what some of the unknown unknown might be for your situation. Be wild, stretch – sometimes the crazy and the implausible stretches into the borders of the unknown, the uncharted but possibly intuited.

"This little map has traveled the globe. It's just a prop, a cosmic swerve, a silly prompt for exploration and celebration of the fertile home territory of learning. It awaits you. Would you like to dialogue with the unknown?"

– Ann Kerwin, creator of the ignorance map

Background

Imagine: A gardener, archaeologist and
astronomer go for a walk...

The iceberg model is used in many contexts. The core premise
is that whatever appears visible, knowable or obvious has deeper
causes that lie beyond our view. These causes play a critical role
in anchoring and sustaining the stuff that we notice. In psychology the unseen drivers might be dubbed the subconscious and in
ecology there's vast networks involved in maintaining sustainable
conditions. The interdependence between the seen and unseen
is also integral to economics, anthropology, politics, population
health- most disciplines interested in understanding systems.

Professor Sohail Inayatullah has been influential in mobilising
the use of the iceberg model through the framework of causal layer
analysis. In his TEDx talk he describes how what we see or notice
is only the tip of much deeper root systems that are mythical, social
and contextually shaped. For example, the path of major highways
in Australia and the United States trace long-existing Indigenous
trade networks and migration paths. Or, as our cultural attitudes
towards nature shift, we appreciate the significance for the hidden
life of trees or mycelium networks. The underlying principle is
that everything is connected and with a little probling beneath the
surface, the power and potency of the interplay between the seen
and unseen become illuminated.

By probing layers we can escape the litany of present conditions
and imagine new futures.

Try it yourself

For this task select or create a metaphorical form that
has seen and unseen structures. Suggested forms:
- An iceberg (small tip visible but significant ballast
  below and unseen, ecosystem conditions e.g. water
  temp, climate, currents)
- A tree (roots, branches, leaves, soil and ecosystem
  qualities e.g. soil, water, light, air)
- Radiating star (drawn from star bursting used in
  business and management)

Pick a problem you are interested in. To help you
gain a range of perspectives take a gardener, an
archeologist and astronomer with you. Each will
help you probe the problem from different angles.

This phase searches for values, underlying beliefs or
conditions that underlie the space you are exploring.

1. Time frame: continuous
What is immediately visible - events; who is involved,
what evidence is being used to tell the story?

2. Time frame: years
What are the causes e.g. short term social, economic,
cultural -shorter term histories and explanations.

3. Time frame: decades
Cultural values, language, organising institutions and
government instruments, prevailing discourse.

4. Time frame: societal/civilisation
Myths and metaphors (archetypes, ancient stories,
gut/ emotional responses).

Asking what, when, where
and why can help probe.
- What has been tried,
  worked, not worked.
- How long, leading
  influences
- Where - context,
  proxy, adjacent
  situation
- Why - root causes,
  preconditions

Andrew Trieu – Metaphors. Waterholes and circles.

Andrew works as a change manager across a range of sectors. He has been developing his thinking on the use of metaphor and building that into his practice. By framing an organization, or sector through metaphor, Andrew creates a space for opening up assumptions that have become set in the sector. While at first the metaphors can feel abstract, it is through looking at an organisation, or a sector "as if it was" that concrete insights begin to emerge.

"The Circle of life symbolizes the universe being sacred and divine. It represents the infinite nature of energy. If something dies it gives new life to another. This spiritual meaning of the circle represents a divine life form, or spirit that keeps our reality in motion.

It is symbolic of vitality, wholeness, completion and perfection. The meaning of shapes and symbols meet us when we are ready to listen and learn. The circle at its core is about relationships, harmony and unity."

Within organisational change management there is a constant tension of managing different perspectives, while building capability and capacity towards desired futures. Within Andrew's practice, the use of metaphor has become increasingly fruitful, and central to his practice. Reflecting on his work in the care sector, Andrew brought together the *Circle of Life* and the *Waterhole* metaphors to create space for creative discussion within his organization.

"The *Circle of Life* and the *Waterhole* make a creative conceptual space to reflect on how our sector creates 'vitality' and 'relationships'. In the living world situation of an African Waterhole, diverse species have come to learn to migrate to the waterhole at a particular moment. Natural predators and symbiotic animals gather around this special place for various significant rituals: to quench their thirst, to mate, to prepare for end of life.

Take for example a herd of elephants, the act of migrating to the waterhole is part of developing memory loops to the baby elephant. A flock of birds is able to travel significant distances, sometimes across continents to congregate at a specific waterhole.

If we flip this context of the waterhole back to an organizational change management context, we begin to ask: Why are we here? What is our purpose? What is the change, and why are we changing?

This may be representative of the 'water' as a boundary object in the waterhole landscape. Who are the stakeholders? What relationships do they hold? What tensions exist? How can they collaborate? What can they contribute?

This may be representative of the 'different species'. What are the behaviors that we want to sustain and embed? What is the culture we want to shape and form? This may be representative of the invisible forces that signal the activation of migration to the waterhole and how we behave at the waterhole and the rituals that take place along and during the journey.

Does the waterhole represent and symbolize *Care*? Care for self, the herd and the offspring? If so, who are we caring for? How do we care? Why do we care?"

visualising

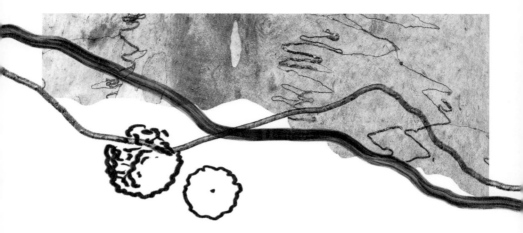

Visualising is much more than seeing – it invites us to tap into immense complexity that marries the anatomical potential of seeing to the rich intersections between our memories, our senses and perceiving anew. Transduction, the biophysical process of turning sensory stimulation into patterns and pathways for responding to life, is an amazing kind of alchemy and visualization helps us consciously tap into the information of texture, light and shadow contrasts, colour, form and space. As the adage 'seeing is believing' implies, we tend to give precedence to vision and in doing so we can short circuit the vast networks of sensory pathways that shape what we see. Our visual cortex alone overlays complex mappings of texture, contrasts, movement and geographic orientation and that's all without the wonder of being able to sense the world in commutations of colour.

It can come as a surprise to realise that what we say we see is often an abstracted composite. We constantly make sense by drawing on shorthand symbols that simultaneously are convenient communicators while also acting as blinkers that shield us from engaging with what is really present. There are times and places for both. By tapping into what we see and how we see with some time worn methods used by visual communicators, we can hone how we make use of this powerful mode of communication.

Background

In much the same way that stretching can help circulation, agility and body memory, there are things we can do to warm up the regions in our brain and hands that are often linked to visualising:

Respond
Flowing with intuition and a first response to drawing or simply making marks can help declutter thoughts and create a relaxing environment.

Repeat
Repeating the same creative exercise with a slight variation in process can help stimulate divergent thinking.

Focus
Focusing on one element that you wouldn't usually emphasise whilst drawing can offer a new perspective.

Try it yourself

For these stretches, you'll need paper and a pen or pencil. Complete each stretch below, spending no more than 3 minutes per stretch:

1. Sit with a partner (any willing creative friend) and draw their face without looking at the page or taking your hand off the paper. Do this quickly – 15 seconds is a good time.
2. Repeat the first stretch but with your other hand. This exercise stimulates the connections between hand, eye and attention for both hemispheres.
3. Repeat the first stretch but with an object near you, rather than a person's face.
4. Take the object from the third stretch and draw it by only drawing the shadows and light reflections. Don't draw the outline. You can shade in areas or draw around the edges of the light and shadow patterns. This exercise tunes up the region of the visual cortex linked to mapping patterns through light and texture.

green LEAVES
SOIL water
roots

plant ROOT
fern LOG dirt
flowers LOG dirt
bark chlorophyll

woodfruit garden
branch SPRING
PLANT twig
PLANT trunk

AUTUMN branches
veins green OXYGEN
evergreen bark
leaves TWIGS

woodland FUNGi green
VINE botany twigs leaves

"A picture is worth a
thousand words."
– Frederick R. Barnard

Background

Part of the reason for this is that there is so much information that can be condensed into an image. In creating visualisations we are reaching into layers of symbolism or a shared metaphorical language that have become consensually understood to stand for and act as short hand signs. Even reading is an act of connecting letters / alphabetical symbols. A quick scan in your environment can reveal a plethora of signs and symbols guiding our attention, shaping our behaviour and echoing generational messages.

Our environments can be experienced from the intimate to more expansive scales. Human habitats are rich with signs and symbols. A quick scan reveals symbols in collections of stationery, piles of paperwork, a wardrobe with shoes, t-shirts and logos, appliances, corridors, footpaths, parks and roadsides. The natural environment is live with signs too but for this exercise, we will limit our gaze to human messaging systems.

Try it yourself

Have a look around your environment and look for signs and symbols that:

- Warn – hazard
- Direct – exit sign
- Identify – logo
- Echo – a cross (medical or religious)

Use a camera or sketch to document your findings.

Photomontage and collage apps are interesting ways to composite your findings. Explore ways in which you can collate your sources and imagery.

Background

Sketching is a particular kind of visualising that can help reveal what we are thinking in real time. Sketching has been found to be useful in clarifying our thoughts and bringing to the surface ideas that are difficult to articulate. The tracks and lines we make through sketching helps us to access spatial, motor and emotional knowledge that we can sense before we can say. Sketching can also act like a conversation with ourselves and equally so, with others.

Designers use sketching to shape and understand each other's ideas – it's a kind of thinking through doing. What might seem like messy marks and strokes on a page is like an echo of thought paths which can be useful to those involved at the time. It also acts as a reminder of the details long after the conversation is over.

Art and cognition researcher Andrea Kantrowitz claims that 40% of the brain is devoted to visual perception and mental imagery, and has found that there can be a constant negotiation between what we know and what we see. Cognition is the combination of mind, body and world experience. Drawing through thinking can be thought of as the process of reflecting in and out. Whilst drawing, we can take in the current moment and bring out our inner experiences at the same time - it can then allow new perspectives or clarifications when combined with another person's process.

Try it yourself

This activity can help you bring ideas to the surface, become more agile in visualising, help discuss and articulate ideas and build memories.

Choose a topic or challenge you would like to explore with someone. Your topic might be conceptual, organisational or spatial – for example:
- How can we think about x
- How do we connect a, b and c so that d and e...
- What if this shape/form/object/idea is placed here or was moved here or we add this

Make sure you each have something to draw with – you can share but it's easier if you both 'sketch' at the same time. Draw over each other's marks, move into different parts of the page, take turns, sketch at the same time, talking aloud as you do so. Don't worry about how good or bad your sketches are, just let your hands act as an extension of your mind.

As you draw, notice how you understand squiggles, build on ideas and recognise what the traces mean.

When you feel that your conversation has reached a conclusion, look back at the marks. What do you notice about gestures: do they show emotions, investments in energy – heavy marks, lots of criss-crossing, shapes? Some people like to draw in pictures, others neat lines and some are circular, emotive and vine like. Are there areas of focus or concentration: spaces, connections, separations, traces of heavy traffic? Can you identify moments where your ideas joined or shifted?

Annotate your drawings. Annotate the sketch at the end with quick notes about where, when and what the conversation involved.

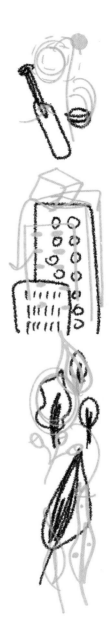

Background

In the same way signs, symbols and sketching can help bring ideas to the surface so too can rich pictures. Rich pictures tap into the language of symbols but they may be less formalised and more linked into the nuances of individual memory and experience.

Rich pictures are useful when working with complex systems and concepts that are hard to define. By using simple, hand drawn pictures, diagrams and interaction loops, contextual meanings and relationships outside of language can rise to the surface. Again, it's not the quality of the drawing but the way the pictures conjure associations, metaphors and shared understandings.

Minimal text/wording can help make the pictures communicate to a wider range of people but the main aim is to visualise complex ideas in a specific context - the reach and broader understanding is not the first priority.

Try it yourself

Rich pictures can be done as rough, cartoon-like drawings or (if you want to stretch out) by using magazine cutouts in a kind of hybrid collage – a good range of magazines is needed to cover a broad range of interests. Collages can also be created digitally using image sources on the net and image programs such as Photoshop. This exercise can also be done in 3D with objects like blocks, lego and plasticine.

Take an organisation or system you are involved with and use rich pictures to show:
- The roles stakeholders/key parties play
- Contextual features such as location, objects or forms of significance
- The direction of interactions and qualities such as energy, power, sensation and time

Your pictures should be understandable to others unfamiliar with your situation. You may want to use arrows and brief annotations to help interpretation.

Background

Exquisite Corpse, or cadavre exquis as it was originally known in French, is an artistic parlour game developed by French Surrealists in the 1920s. The process involves collectively developing a composition where each section is developed by a different person, with each contributor only able to see a small portion of the previously created section of the work. The results help us to find non-linear connections while revealing diverse ways of seeing that stir subconscious memories into action. Never doubt how a game can be fertile ground for the emergence of new ideas!

The Surrealist poet Simone Kahn describes the game as "a system, a method of research, a means of delightful, fantastic drama as well as stimulation, and even, perhaps, a kind of drug".

Try it yourself

Get a group of 2-4 colleagues or friends together. Take a rectangular piece of paper and fold it so there are as many sections as there are participants.

Set a short timer (1-3min) for the first participant to sketch something on the top section of paper. The participant may want to draw some connecting lines into the next section as well, for the next participant.

Once they are finished, fold it so that the first participant's sketch cannot be seen. Repeat this process for each of the participants. At the end, unfold and marvel at your exquisite corpse! Are there any unexpected similarities or differences between the sections?

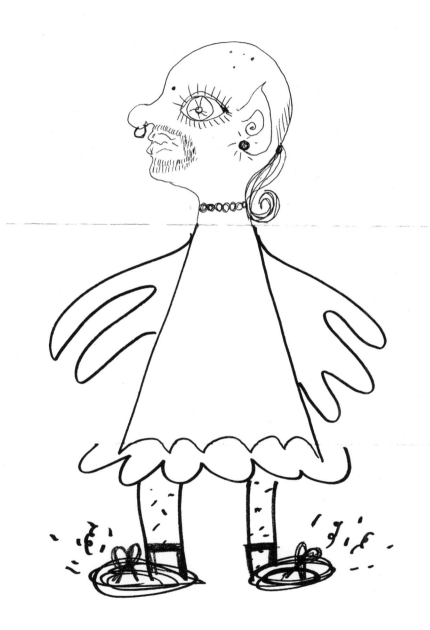

Background

Movement mapping is a method that is used by designers for space and motion tracking. This method has been used by a myriad of practitioners including geographers, economists, engineers, physiotherapists, landscape designers, architects, urban planners, traffic strategists, choreographers along with scenographers and directors of stage and screen. These practitioners have harnessed the dynamics of movements in space. Movement maps can be generated for dynamics that occur in 2D, 3D and 4D, whether it's macro and micro contexts. Maps can cover continents, time, bodies, cultural trends, interior processes and molecular exchanges. Some subjects to map can include ideas, dancers, traffic, planetary, changed air travel during covid, light in parks or muscle rehabilitation.

MIT's Computer Science and AI Laboratory have developed a technique called Mosculp, which uses video inputs of humans moving through space to create a 3D render of their motion. They've demonstrated Mosculp by capturing the movements of various athletes, from basketball players to distance runners to ballet dancers.

Scan the QR code for some fascinating movement maps.

Try it yourself

For this exercise pick a subject and with a moving dynamic that would have practical application to your context. Look for the following on a single plane (i.e. in 2D) that represents a vertical, horizontal or a diagonal slice through space:

· Changes in states
· Directions in flows
· Absences
· Rhythms
· Clusters and overlays
· Shapes
· Intensity

If you have time and interest, experiment with several different planes by creating a map for each dynamic separately. Represent each with a different colour or line (e.g. dotted, solid, hyphen-ated line) and provide a legend. Your map can be hand drawn or generated with a drawing app.

Some tips: Use the same scale and create fixed reference points. This helps you compare your data/findings. You can use a blank page folded into grids, graph paper, print and copy a photograph or sketch a copy for each. Alternatively use tracing paper over the image. This gives you the option to overlay, compare and look for emergent patterns.

Having completed these observations, what have you noticed? If you could change one feature what would it be and how would you do it?

Background

Being able to appreciate visual language and use it creatively can be like entering a world of never ending possibility which brings the world alive moment to moment. It also fosters our ability to synthesize rather than analyse, to see relationships in seemingly disconnected fields, find broad patterns rather than answers and call on the ability of the brain's right hemisphere to bring together simultaneous contextual information.

The Gestalt theory was developed in the 1930s by German psychologists Max Wertheimer, Kurt Koffka and Wolfgang Kohler. They were interested in understanding how people create meaningful perceptions in a chaotic world of stimuli. The theory is used as a form of psychotherapy although it's also a tool for creativity. It relates to how we interpret shapes, patterns and configurations in our environment and thoughts.

We can group together similar elements within a complex image to gain a better understanding of it overall. It's a navigation tool between our environment and our response. This helps us discover meaning, although it can also cause an auto-pilot effect too, so it helps to look for new details or stand back to gain a new perspective. Tuning into personal experiences and staying aware of patterns or assumptions can also help regulate personal responses.

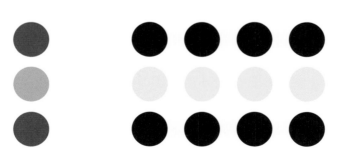

Using the principles of Gestalt helps us explore the way we have integrated patterns through complex and polysensory pathways channelled through our visual cortex circuits. In playing with gestalt principles we can discover the way specialised neurons (feature detectors) respond to specific dynamics such as:

- Horizontal and vertical lines that are signalled in contrasts of light and dark
- Direction
- Colour
- Contrast
- Texture

We can also consider how the visual cortex also relays signals to other regions of the brain that specialise in:

- What - shape, colour and texture maps that look for changes in shape based on pre-exisitng memories of pattern.
- Where - space, tracking in size and shifts in the background while looking for objects in space (important for guiding movement and kinaesthetic awareness).

Wertheimer, Koffka and Kohler established a set of principles that are involved in making sense of what and how we see. The Gestalt is everywhere and permeates experience from the intimate to expansive. While we might be tempted to seek the Gestalt through our eyes, we can tune in through other realms of sensation. When we apply the principles of the Gestalt we may find many principles to be present at the same time. Each is acting in a symphony of sensation between our physical experiences and cognitive capacities as we navigate the world. In attending to the world through the filters of each principle we can endlessly notice shifting patterns and become more aware of how particular assemblages make us feel. This enables us to become adept in identifying how tweaks (both small and/or big) can have far reaching impacts.

Gestalt principles

Closure (Reification)
Preferring complete shapes, we automatically fill in gaps between elements to perceive a complete image; so, we see the whole first.

Common Region
We group elements that are in the same closed region.

Meaningfulness (Familiarity)
We group elements if they form a meaningful or personally relevant image.

Regularity
Sorting items, we tend to group some into larger shapes, and connect any elements that form a pattern.

Figure/Ground
Disliking uncertainty, we look for solid, stable items. Unless an image is truly ambiguous, its foreground catches the eye first.

Common Fate
We group elements that move in the same direction.

Prägnanz
We perceive complex or ambiguous images as simple ones.

Similarity (Invariance)
We seek differences and similarities in an image and link similar elements.

Good Form
We differentiate elements that are similar in colour, form, pattern, etc. from others—even when they overlap—and cluster them together.

Element Connectedness
We group elements linked by other elements.

Proximity (Emergence)
We group closer-together elements, separating them from those farther apart.

Symmetry
We seek balance and order in designs, struggling to do so if they aren't readily apparent.

Try it yourself

Pick 5 of the Gestalt principles. Have a look out of a window and notice each principle in objects in the outside world – you'll be surprised at how easy it is to see the principles at play. In your creative journal, note what principles you see and what you see them in.

Over the next day, pick pauses between your activities or daily rituals to note your selected principles at play in your environments (e.g work, home, exercise, recreations, etc). For each principle below go on a scavenger hunt with your phone and look for examples of each. Paste the images you take into your journal and annotate them with the principles at play.

Extend your range. Pick three arrangements from the list below and filter them with the 5 principles you have selected. This time, use your imagination to visualise some of the principles. Using your selected Gestalt principles create a set of small cards (loose A6). For each principle draw out the principle from the photo, use two colours (e.g black and white can generate powerful contrasts) and turn the principle into contrasting shapes. At the end you will have 5 cards. Play with putting them in different sequences/ configurations. Look for an opportunity to alter your original arrangement e.g. could the meal be presented differently? Could a haircut be modified?

- A meal
- A beverage
- A piece of music
- An interior
- A page or website
- A landscape (natural or designed)

- A shop
- A perfume
- A shoe design
- A haircut
- Something of your own choosing

Portrait

Background

A portrait is a detailed study. Spending time to sit with and really notice the details before you is a kind of immersive way of bringing attention and interaction together. It is also a way to see the big picture and the way the elements or parts can come together through summoning our intuitive understanding to bring things together.

For a portrait to take on qualities of the whole it needs to tap into the relationships between relationships – those non linear qualities that bring parts into symphony. It involves drawing what you see, not what you remember. This is different from using symbols or rich pictures – it is about working with shadow, light, gradation, absences, looking for shapes and the way they connect or merge.

There are many ways in which portraits have been created throughout time and culture. Drawings and paintings of people tend to come to mind and they can be powerful ways of tapping into the wide range of phenomena at play – shifting light, emotional gestures, identity expressions – the worlds within and without. Landscapes, still lives, flora and fauna portraits are equally rich forms of portraiture. Portraits can be created through all kinds of media including pencil sketches, paintings, sculpture/3D, musical and textural. There are also a myriad of culturally specific practices such as dot painting, weaving, beading and dance.

Try it yourself

For the purpose of this exercise choose a portrait subject and medium that you can visualise.

Don't worry about your expertise, the real value is in the time you spend and the detail that emerges. You can do this in a single sitting or over a series of intervals though some elements will shift. An hour will provide a good degree of detail though portraits can be quite luring and may draw you in for a longer haul.

Here are some tips:
- Try drawing upside down
- Start with shadows and reflections and sketch softly
- Roughly block out the light and dark regions
- Look for the shape of dints, furrows, dips and raised section
- Sketch in angles and proportions
- Draw with different eyes
- Blur your eyes
- Use a mirror

Lee Wallace – Movement Mapping.

"Rape and sexualised assault are under-reported." These seven words, put together in this certain way make a statement that is as undeniable as it is complex.

We've become accustomed to crime being solved. Our prisons have never been fuller. So why are we worried about rape? Lee took her decades of experience in policy and innovation and focussed on this question.

"Victim-survivors are often silenced by perpetrators, or the systems that are meant to protect them. Silence comes from a real fear that they will not be believed or will be victim-blamed further adding to barriers to engage with the system.

They're described as wearing the wrong clothes, or drinking too much and so the blame is on them. Silence is normalised in the community as it is an uncomfortable conversation that most would rather ignore. This silence allows for the emergence of a cultural acceptance of rape and violence."

Lee used some new tools to make sense of this and in so doing reframed the issue.

"I used Movement Mapping to visually represent the national reporting and conviction rates of rape and sexualised assault. I took time to think about it and make a graph. I put rates on the Y-axis and reporting and convictions on the X-axis.

I was using coloured pencils that are soft and a little crumbly, which allowed 'broad' marks to fill the space in each column quickly choosing different colours to differentiate columns made it easier to read and understand with a glance.

Pondering what this last column might be, I quickly realised the common theme was trauma. And trauma was pervasive, reported or not, and whether there was a conviction. As I started to colour, imagining an entire column of trauma representing 100 per cent, my colouring did not stop. The pervasiveness of trauma spread as I coloured above reporting, unreported and convictions columns. It did not stop there.

I coloured above and below, completing every uncoloured space, driving home that trauma was pervasive of the whole civic and justice ecosystems. The act of colouring revealed the extent of the trauma. My physical body did the work, and I saw the result on the page in front of me."

What difference did it make?

If the system can't deal with it, then we need a new system. The current system is failing. It's not just that it isn't working to achieve justice, it is perpetuating the trauma and contributing to its own failure to uphold justice.

In reaching this insight Lee has shifted her thinking from being bounded within the current system. The current criminal justice systems weren't made with rape and sexualised violence in mind, or at least, not front of mind. We have many different types of courts that are purpose specific (Industrial, Children, Family, Criminal, Civil, etc.) what if we had a purpose made system for rape and sexualised violence? What kind of system would we need to shift from rape and sexualised violence being rarely reported, to making them rare?

scaling

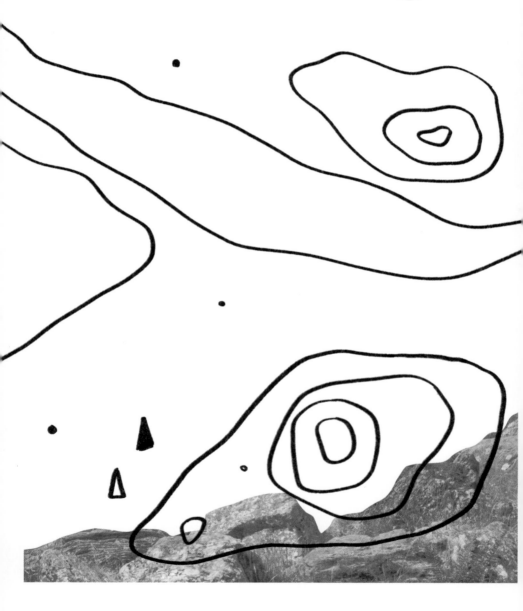

"In every grain of sand there is a story of the earth." — Rachel Carson, Marine Biologist & Conservationist

Scale is a powerful way to stretch our imaginations, assumptions and find ourselves in an ever expanding, ever moving cosmos of possibilities. As the industrial age has shown us, being able to scale up has tapped into the dynamics of creation, destruction and a deeper understanding of living processes. Our experiments and manipulations of scale have lent towards extractive growth but equally so a wider range of lenses can help us make new links between living systems and macro and micro interactions. This series of experiments can help reveal limitations, boundary shifts and unseen patterns of connection.

Background

Scale is a dynamic that intersects across multiple domains and in different ways. We often hear scale referred to in organising practices particularly as notions of growth and retraction - scaling up, scale down.

Playing with scale can reveal the simple rules that shape assumptions, values and potential ramifications or unintended consequences. Looking for simple rules can reveal patterns that we carry through from the past and be useful in testing how things fit together in localised contexts as we imagine possible futures.

In 1986 computer graphics artist Craig Reynolds developed a program to animate a collection of shapes on screen. By combining three simple rules, the emergent behaviour of the shapes remarkably mimics the real life flocking behaviour of birds.

Scan the QR code to see a clip about how simple rules create dynamic patterns.

Try it yourself

Use one or more of the prompts below to kick off
your thinking around scale and rules. Jot down
your thoughts and look to use a range of media
to record your experiments e.g. sketches, images,
collages, formulas.

- Take something that is a small, recurring part of your life and
  increase its use significantly. For example, take a morning cup
  or coffee – what if everyone drank coffee like water 2-3 litres
  per day?

- Play the magician: magnify, shrink or eliminate a structure,
  system, organising behaviour or thing. E.g. car parks, an agricul-
  tural system, an insect, a house, a planet.

- Create giants and microbes: imagine if dinosaurs still walked the
  planet. How would that impact things? Take something very small
  and make it huge – what happens?

- Take a part or unit or system, repeat it while keeping it uniform or
  predictable as possible – e.g. create a new kind of Big Mac burger,
  medical panacea like Panadol, a flavour like vanilla essence.

- Take a pattern or dynamic that seems naturally occurring,
  rhythmic and sequential and disturb it with a random intervention or with a new recurring intervention. Think seasons, the 60
  minute hour, aging.

- Take something that seems like a cornerstone of daily activity and
  make it extinct or a relic of the past.

- Create an intervention from the solar system/out of space.

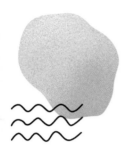

Background

Living systems form patterns linked to movement, distinction and chance. They can be found at microscopic and macroscopic scales and are increasingly used in biomimicry and morphogenesis.

Morphogenesis refers to living processes that influence the shape, size or colour of the natural world – processes that have since been emulated in design ranging across practices such as architecture, textiles, engineering, medicine and digital media.

These biological processes interest artists: designers, engineers and scientists as looking to mimic elements of nature's systems helps with responding to problems or creating new things that are environmentally synergistic. This approach is known as biomimicry. Products you interact with every day benefit from biomimicry. For example, velcro was designed in the 1940s by studying the structure of plant burrs. More recently, the unique properties of shark skin have been used to develop swimsuits that reduce drag.

Replicating patterns are often distilled in mathematics. They can give rise to amazing patterns that can be expressed as concrete forms but it is equally beguiling to consider how they change and the qualities that differentiate living and non living processes.

Mathematical patterns can be found across nature too. Hexagonal patterns recur in honeycomb, snowflakes, and bubble clusters, while a shape known as the fibonacci spiral has been found across diverse biomes in seashells and flowers.

Prompt.
Can think of any other mathematical or geometrical expressions that might have manifestations in the natural world?

Try it yourself

Using your camera phone go on a hunt for:
- Spirals
- Branching
- Hexagons
- Waves
- Cracks
- Stripes
- Spots
- Meandering paths/curves

While you go about this activity look for:
- Moments of chance
- The material state (liquid, solid)
- Direction and rates of movement
- Symmetry, asymmetry, moving, static
- Mathematical/formula or geometrical representations

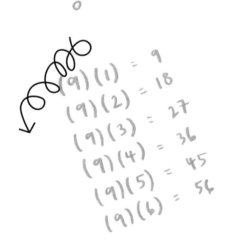

$$(9)(1) = 9$$
$$(9)(2) = 18$$
$$(9)(3) = 27$$
$$(9)(4) = 36$$
$$(9)(5) = 45$$
$$(9)(6) = 56$$

Background

By honing in on the windows of time we pay attention to, we have been able to move people and mountains. There can be a tendency to simplify and reduce but this can be restrictive if not risky. Inasmuch as there is magic to playing with time we have also learnt that the call to consider the context and consequences is omnipresent. As we consider our place on the planet, an appreciation for how the past, present and future intersect become increasingly critical to our adaptive capacities. By taking a simple sliver of our daily life along with our imaginations, we can travel metamorphic evolutionary cycles.

Scan the QR code to see a graphic story of how the earth looked at different points in time. Consider how all of the objects around you originate in elements that were present in the universe millions of years ago, and will continue to have a kind of presence far into the future!

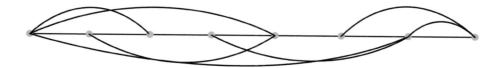

Try it yourself

Pick an object on your desk/work area and:

Consider the tools, technology and materials involved in making this object..
Working backwards, consider the object's life in reverse time:
I year ago, IO years ago, IOO years, IOOO years, etc.
Now do this as a future time process: where will it be in I year, IO years, IOO, IOOO?

Some features you might wish to focus:
- What is it made from?
- Where might the materials have come from?
- What evolutionary processes were involved?
- What industrial processes were involved?
- Are there historical or cultural factors that influenced their design?
- What if we didn't have access to this – think of 5 processes that might not work?
- Think of a way that this could cause havoc or chaos?
- How will this part decay? **Scan the QR to zoom in on a pen.**

Background

Time-lapse and long exposure photography can capture motion that occurs over time scales too large or too small for humans to experience in day to day life. These technologies can help us to see temporal dynamics stretching across geographical and microscopic scales. Surfacing these hidden traces and densities help us to see human centred experiences amidst a much wider range of patterns and resource movements in ways that could previously only have been 'felt' or measured at intervals. The first set of photographs that captured a sequence in time were produced by Eadweard Muybridge, who wanted to demonstrate to others the mechanics of a horse in motion. Cinema and animation intersect with time-lapse as they also stitch together moments in time and capture our imaginations. In the case of time-lapse, it is the scale and focus on a specific dynamic that offers a point of difference.

In a short article explaining the history of time-lapse photography, Wallis Seaton comments on the aspects of movement that emerge through time-lapse:

" Time-lapse started out as sequence photography dating back to experiments in the 1870's. The aims remain the same - to study movement patterns by isolating segments and speeding them up."

Wallis Seaton - Time-lapse Photography: old and new technology.

The invisible motion of aging

Aging is a process you can feel happening but can't see. Filmmaker Anthony Cerniello created a fascinating 'time-lapse' by taking photos of a friend's family members, and then working with CGI animators to animate a progression between the portraits.

Read more about the process behind the film in an article in Colossal and watch the video in full by scanning the QR code.

Try it yourself

Make a video of a range of actions at different speeds: in slow motion, time lapse, real time, photo burst. Keep the audio on.

Compile them. What does it reveal? What new insights emerge? Do you notice speed, frequency, density, energy, transformations in shape, subtle shifts at the edges, transitions in colour and light, patterns of reverberation and rhythm?

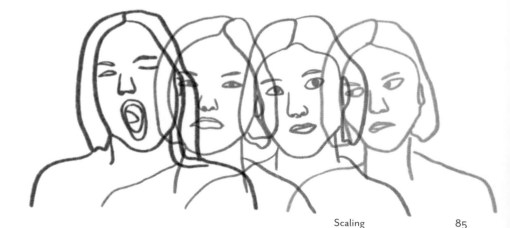

Background

Messages were once passed by drumming patterns across mountain ranges - they were called message drums. Over time we have developed all kinds of communications systems such as morse code, telegraphs and radio that leap frog physical and temporal scales.

The language of computer coding is one such example. At its core, our cyber network is based in binary language. With the click of buttons we mobilize vast fields of data chunked together in compressed binary bundles. The scales involved are barely tangible and yet they profoundly shape our physical worlds.

A language of contrasts

Binary language is a simple language of contrast, of 'ons' and 'offs' or presence and absence. Living systems and their replications are complex and dynamic aggregations of contrast.

Noticing contrast at different scales helps identify nuances in the rates of movement, different kinds of relationships and energy exchanges. As you send messages using the internet, look to notice how these technologies help us bridge scale. At the same time, consider the kinds of information that might be lost and gained.

For an interesting perspective on the energy it takes to send and sort emails scan the QR code.

Try it yourself

In this exercise you are invited to make physical and tangible binary coding as a way of slowing down and surfacing the digital language that underpins so much of our lives.

Use the ASCII code table to write or clap (0 is not sound) your name in binary code.

Create a binary code (use ASCII lower case) log book of the people you meet with over a day.

Ask each person for a story about their name.

Notice how the extended time with each other creates a space for other kinds of exchange (e.g. random conversation, reading body language, tone of voice, memories).

At the end of the day reflect on some of the losses and gains linked to reaching across time in terms of:
· Compression
· Expansion
· Speed
· Intimacy

ASCII Alphabet			
A	1000001	N	1001110
B	1000010	O	1001111
C	1000011	P	1010000
D	1000100	Q	1010001
E	1000101	R	1010010
F	1000110	S	1010011
G	1000111	T	1010100
H	1001000	U	1010101
I	1001001	V	1010110
J	1001010	W	1010111
K	1001011	X	1011000
L	1001100	Y	1011001
M	1001101	Z	1011010

Background

Charles and Ray Eames' 'Powers of Ten' changed the way designers worked with the world. In a ground breaking video, the idea of interaction, change and continuity across scale became championed and a go to tool for design. The insights that emerge through considering relationships across scale are increasingly revealing and insight provoking.

The film, 'Powers of Ten' was so acclaimed that in 1998 it was selected for preservation in the United States National Film Registry as being "culturally, historically, or aesthetically significant".

The film depicts an adventure in magnitudes. It takes us on a journey around the universe by moving through space and time every ten seconds. It starts off as a small moment on Earth then zooms out to the galaxy, until we are just a speck.

'Scale of the Universe' is an interactive website similar to the 'Powers of Ten'. By scrolling in and out you can view the relative sizes of various objects in the universe, or click to learn about objects. **Scan the QR to learn more about the 'Powers of Ten' and the work of Charles and Ray Eames.**

Try it yourself

Pick something from your environment that you would like
to enrich by expanding your range of perception. It could
be habitual space that is almost mundane or seemingly
insignificant. It could be something that provokes strong
sensations such as fascination, joy, annoyance or frustration Use this as your starting point and create an image
grid, a video or slide show that is inspired by Eames,
'Power of Ten'.

Things that might help:
- Get inspiration online from images taken by satellites
  or through microscopes
- Use a magnifying glass
- Play with different lenses - even reading glasses, glass
  spheres, the bottom of drinking glasses
- Capture images through water
- Flip binoculars around - use you phone camera to
  take photos from each end
- If you have access to a telescope you can place your
  phone camera over the view finder
- Photograph the same object/ space at 10 cm intervals -
  zooming out from the closest point of focus

"The material of music is sound and silence. Integrating these is composing." – John Cage

Background

Music is a wonderful medium to encounter and consider scale. Music channels our emotional spectrum and moves our bodies into moments of both solitary contemplation and impassioned shared activity. Music marries sound and creative expression, it can ground wavelengths and ranges of audible vibration. Music takes us through journeys of culture, history and place while spanning technologies for creation, recording and performance. It takes us into relationships with all manner of other music makers in the spectrum of life – birds, crickets, whales, rock surfaces, forest floors and the sounds of the skies.

Brian Eno has been a long term player in creating and reflecting on how music mediates our experiences of time and place. He has worked on all manner of projects which explore feelings and music. His work is a great source of creative stimulation.

Scale and complexity in its multiple interpretations can be encountered through music, as David Byrne so neatly discusses in the first chapter of his book 'How Music Works'.

For inspiration search 'iconic album covers designs'. There are a wide range of seminal covers that bring together experimental new-age artworks and musical journeys. **Scan the QR codes for ideas.**

Try it yourself

Create a playlist of music. This could be made on Spotify, iTunes or another music platform. Then develop an artwork that visually expresses what the playlist is about. Think about how to conjure a sense of scale.

It is up to you how you interpret 'scale' but look to:
- Name your album
- Provide a one liner that helps listeners grasp your curatorial decisions

You can decide to make your work in multiple ways with various elements. It could either be a mood board for a production company rather than a finished graphic design or a single mock up of an album cover.

In curating your album you may wish to consider:
- The environment/ space/ room the music was made for
- The instruments – materials, technologies and performance
- Cultural context – contemplative, collective, for dance, for ceremony, power – for whom
- Era – when, where, historical influences
- Inspiration – natural, emotional and mythical archetypes
- Patterns, rhythms, shifts, surprises

Source recommendations: see the website for templates, layouts and inspiration sources such as:
- Canva - designing layouts
- Pinterest

"Music resonates in so many parts of the brain that we can't conceive of it being an isolated thing. It's whom you were with, how old you were, and what was happening that day." — David Byrne, quote from How Music Works

Background

Memory boards or message sticks are touch stories or mnemonic devices that help transmit encyclopaedias of knowledge across scale. They can also be created as strings of beads or belts. There is a connection to practices that involve telling about the land and aural culture, that are deeply intertwined with place.

The lukasa is usually made up of beads and shells arranged strategically on a block of wood. A skilled lukasa reader will use the arrangement of the lukasa as a mnemonic prompt to retell and pass on the Luba kingdom's history and culture.

The lukasa isn't the only example of how indigenous practices encode memory and knowledge linked to place. Aboriginal Australian songlines draw on the land as a mnemonic device to record and pass down cultural stories accrued over millennia.

Scan the QR code to listen to a podcast where Lynne Kelly shares her research into how songlines encode detailed information about a place in song.

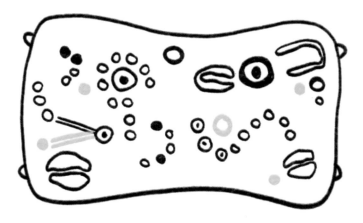

Your task

Part 1: Start your memory board

Go for a walk. Stop at regular intervals (for example: 5-10 stops, ten metres apart).

At each stop, look at a part of the area:
- Close up
- Then something midscale
- Finally, something on horizon

For each scale find something physical either from the area or in your belongings, such as a twig, a button, a bottle cap, a dried leaf, etc.

This becomes the material for your memory board. Find a way to secure it (e.g. glue onto a surface, thread onto string, layer into bottle).

Part 2: Grow your memory board

Repeat the walks over several days (you can also do this over longer time scales e.g. months, seasons, years).

As you go on these repeated walks, link a new piece of knowledge to each location and physical marker on your board. It could be an extra layer of detail – for example, a stick which connects to a leaf which connects to a bud or insect. It can also be a conversation or something you say that stays with you e.g. 'where I talked to my son about dancing' or 'that stick where I heard a bird'.

Each time you add to your memory board, tell the story of connections out loud. If you can share the story with someone else, even better. How might they add to it and build their own?

Carl Heise – The power of music.

Business architecture can be a relatively abstract concept. For Carl, a leader within a large transport agency, helping people to understand business architecture so that they could then engage in the process was an important first challenge. Carl drew on his history as a High-school drama teacher, where he worked with students to stage many live performances. He also drew on framing tools, to create a space where people in his team, and in his organization could collaboratively build the business architecture function.

Carl playfully framed business architecture as if it were the film score of Star Wars. In creating this conceptual space, people in the organization were invited to see the various functions within the organization as elements of the film score.

"We wanted to create something to bring the pieces together and make music. Music can help lift us to an aspirational state. The metaphor helped people see the organisational 'jigsaw' pieces as a 'musical score'.

This helped us to facilitate the conversations, starting with a shared language to bring the 'musical score' to life."

The abstraction of the business architecture function into a film score opened the space for people to see themselves as being part of a complex system.

"If we look at ourselves as a cross-functional musical team we can see that the connected parts of the systems are formed for a particular purpose. In a film score there is a vision and a purpose, with various viewpoints of this vision.

There are many parts to the score, and not every instrument plays the same notes, or at the same time."

Looking at a large organisation as if it is a film score then invites people to see the performance of the score, as the running of the organization. There are many roles within a film score, and within the performance of the score.

"The score gives us a method to communicate the when, how, and why, conducting the purpose through the system. The conductor needs to work with experts, and make the whole bigger and better."

Having created the space for discussion Carl and his team then used the space to collaboratively build and position their function within the organization.

"Architecture is the building plan. This plan then shows us what we need to see, from each of the relevant viewpoints. It articulates the purposes and perspectives across the organization. It also creates business assets that can be used, reused and scaled. The architecture can then also be seen as building blocks."

Having created this conversation Carl and his team then set about building a shared understand how quality is defined within the organization. This then provides the opportunity to have important discussions like "how do we know if a change is an improvement?"

"We want to build a culture that engages people in the process of continuous improvement and models and maintains business knowledge."

conversations

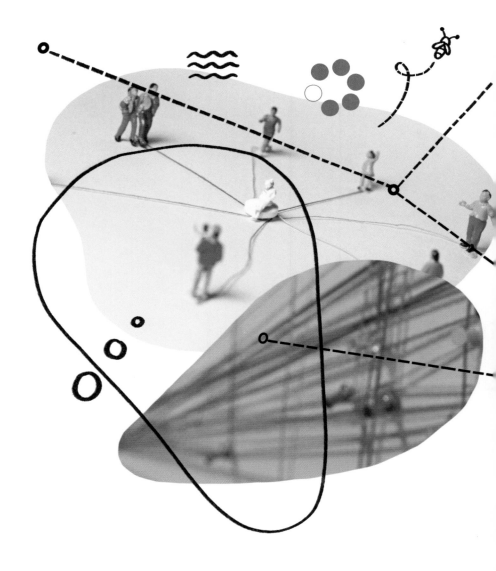

We are communal creatures and we have developed a myriad of ever-changing ways to connect. Communication is a wonderful and varied adaptation that acts as a conduit for our exchanges. Communication has been linked to biological and psychological nourishment – it's a kind of social grooming that fulfils our need to feel connected. Evolutionary research points to the important co-development of our vocal chords in tandem to tool manipulation, which amplified our motivations to collaborate. Being able to convey intentions and mobilise collective action lies at the heart of good experience. Much of this we know intrinsically and can take for granted. There are many ways in which we communicate and if we are searching to enrich our creativity there are lots of tricks we can use to enrich how we 'do' communication, make new connections and perceive anew.

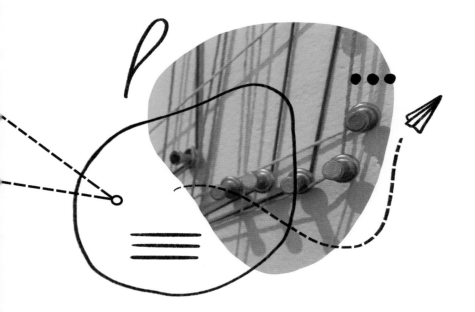

Small talk

Background

Often dismissed as shallow and inconsequential, small talk is part of many meaningful exchanges and social rituals. Small talk sets the vibe, breaks the ice and creates a space for reading a range of subtle cues linked to mood, intention and personal or cultural predispositions. We tune in through posture, facial expression, vocal tone, gestures, body space, agreements on touch, symbolism (e.g. through clothing and furnished environments).

Small talk often joins us in the broad-brush stuff that connects as humans: food, weather, family, sleep. It is adaptive bonding, part of resilience, communal but individually negotiated.

Dr. Justine Coupland is a sociolinguistic expert. In her book, 'Small Talk', she examines the powerful and affirming effects that small talk has in social interactions. She writes, "Small talk cannot be dismissed as peripheral, marginal or minor discourse. Small talk is a means by which we negotiate interpersonal relationships".

A creative small talk conversation
'Dear Data' was a year-long analogue data drawing project by information designers Giorgia Lupi and Stefanie Posavec. Every day, the pair would send each other a postcard featuring a visualisation of some piece of personal data about their daily lives. In this way, the 'Dear Data' project is small talk turned into a shared artefact. For more inspiration search 'Dear Data' online.

Try it yourself

Create a coding system that records types of small talk in your world.

Things to look for:
- The number of conversations
- Themes of conversation: gossip, hobbies, interests
- Moments of kindness
- Tone of conversation (excited, blunt, instructive)
- Motivations for connection (formal and informal)
- Snippets of overheard or unseen conversation

A day of small talk:

WHO IT WAS WITH...
- Work Colleague
- Mum
- Friend
- Child

WHERE IT TOOK PLACE...
home   park   cafe   work   shops

HOW DID IT MAKE ME FEEL...
awkward
excited
bored
curious
sadness

THEMES OF CONVERSATION...
- food
- studies
- health
- music
- sport

Background

A wide range of social connections helps to generate empathy and enhanced appreciation for diversity. By interacting with a diverse range of people we enhance our capacities and motivation to make a difference by helping others, this is a critical factor in long term satisfaction and self esteem.

Proxemics refers to the study of human use of space and its effects on human communication and behaviour. It's a method of inquiry that is useful to many including human geographers, designers of public space, educators negotiating interaction, psychologists working with interpersonal dynamics and performance semioticians/dramaturgs.

One of the earliest researchers in proxemics was Edward Hall, who posited that in Western culture there are four main types of distance people keep: intimate (0 to 45cm), personal (45cm to 1.2m), social (1.2m to 3m), and public (over 3m). This is an average of USA, Canada, Europe and Australia. This distance is socially learned, so these distances as well as levels of physical contact may vary between cultures. He also wrote about how body language, touch and eye contact reveals information about the level of familiarity between people.

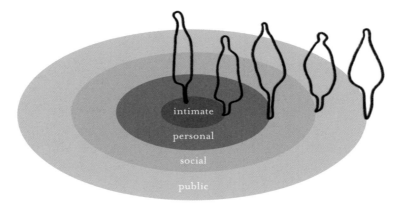

Try it yourself

Map out the spaces where you observe connection with different people in your world. Include connections you are part of, those you witness (are included in but not an active contributor), and those you observe from afar.

Look for the significant to the less visible. Think CEO to cleaner in a work context, or in your neighborhood small children to elders to community connectors such as cafe or local business owners. Each will occupy a role and perspective which bear witness to the worlds you inhabit. Look for interactions across gender, age and cultural background. You might also look for the role animals or objects play in stimulating interactions.

Create two maps:
- A map of where social interactions occurred in the space you observed
- A social distance map/social space circle noting the role space and distance played during interactions

You may like to print out a section of a map and annotate it by hand, or sketch the map out yourself.

Use the social space circle to make notes:
- How many people were involved?
- Were there rituals involved e.g. greetings, farewells?
- Did interactions seem:
  - Random (e.g. seemingly unrelated) or spontaneous (e.g. in the bathroom)?
  - Habitual or part of a daily ritual (e.g. in the kitchen, at the dog park)?
  - Formally organised – e.g. offices and meeting spaces?
  - Informal – e.g. cleaners/service roles
  - Familiar - we are more likely to acknowledge people we have seen often particularly in social contexts we feel less sure about.

Background

We are performing and interactive creatures. Our connections to each other are nourishing, informing, equalising and actively engage us in perspective shifting. We are wired for learning through conversation: mirror neurons are specialised to help us mimic a wide range of behaviours including facial expression and posture.

We are deeply in conversation with our environments through our bodies. We sense and reverberate with the social world. David Linden has researched this embodied communication widely. In his book 'Touch', he shows that sports teams that engage in forms of touch like high fives, hugs and back-pats have greater co-operation and success as a team.

David McNeil (psychologist) makes a special case for the role of gesturing in communicating. He argues that gesturing is fundamentally linked to processing ideas and the ability to express them in language. We often think with our hands – moving our hands helps us think and remember. Gesturing fills in the gaps, dramatizes and brings to life qualities that haven't been spoken.

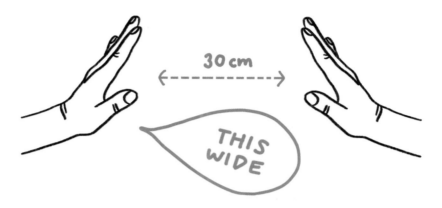

Try it yourself

Observe conversations and interactions over an hour.
Write down your observations and note:
- What postures are used?
- Is posture mimicked or used to shape interactions?
- How is gesture used to fill in gaps or add explanation?
- How often do people mimic facial, vocal and emotional expressions?
- How do gesture and touch come to connect people and/or objects?

Some other things to consider include:
- **Pay attention to gestures alone:** closed and controlled, deliberate, energized, demonstrating action and direction. Watch for the smiles, frown, shifts in posture and body direction.
- **Vocal tone:** Mood, personality, intention, interest, and energy?
- **Facial expression and body:** mirroring patterns or responsive dances (one person does one thing and the other responds in a corresponding but different way).

Background

Denotation and connotation are terms that are most commonly associated with linguistics. However over time the notion of what constitutes text has shifted towards a model of multimodality. In other words, the world around us is imbued with messages and assemblages that speak, guide and are reshaped in nonverbal language that is both physical, personal and interpersonal.

Multimodal communication interests designers of space, systems, services and experiences and increasingly disciplines that explore sense making such as linguistics, philosophy and social sciences. Our living environments are shaped by material decisions that have been explicitly conceived by designers and implicitly by decisions that appear less conscious. Either way they shape, often invisibly, the atmospheres of our habitats, our thoughts and imaginations.

A interesting example of the power of connotation is the design of car horns to appeal to buyers. Car companies are careful to match the sound of car horns to the 'personality' of the car, with BMW even hiring Hollywood composer Hans Zimmer to advise on the horn sounds of their electric vehicles.

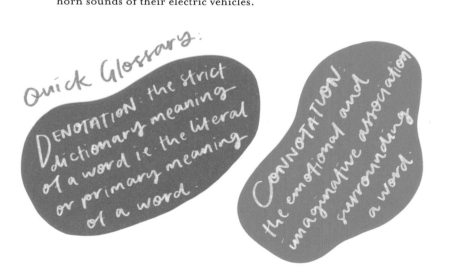

Quick Glossary:

DENOTATION: the strict dictionary meaning of a word ie. the literal or primary meaning of a word.

CONNOTATION: the emotional and imaginative association surrounding a word.

Try it yourself

This exercise is designed to bring the language of materials into focus and highlight both the latent power that is equally alive with creative potential and sly manipulations.

Photograph three materials:
- From your home; routine journey from your home (work, shops, gym, etc); another environment you regularly spend time in
- Put each picture into a column
- Provide a definition for connotation and denotation

Play with switching the materials around e.g. fluffy pink slippers and white bathroom tiles. Don't worry about being logical. What happens to the meanings? Continue to play about with other material combinations. What do you notice about the way that behaviour and pointers towards meanings shift?

Using these insights intentionally create a combination that is really uncomfortable, inappropriately indulgent, cosy or luxurious.

Reflect on your creation. Look for ways this play with materials is used in film, visual merchandising, theatre, festivals, fashion and other design contexts to shift imaginations and conjure stories. Does this prompt you to make changes elsewhere in the worlds you inhabit?

MATERIAL:

ornamental material | cosy, warm

D C   D C   D C

PLAY WITH MEANING

NEW MEANING:
Soft yellow bathroom tiles

Background

Our hands play a key role in bringing us into contact with the world, they help us interact materially and physically. We are more often than not, in constant conversation with our environments via our hands with complex layers of information shaping what we perceive we can do, what we remember and trialing where we might go. Every time you open something (a door, a lid, a zip, a window), notice what your hands are telling you.

With extensive and specialised nerve receptors, our hands are the most integrated part of our anatomy and are linked to multiple intelligences including kinaesthetic, tactile, emotional and spatial. Moreover, using our hands enhances memory, synthesis and our capacity to communicate.

Neurologist Frank R Wilson has studied the role of our hands extensively. In his book 'The Hand. How Its Use Shapes the Brain, Language, and Human Culture' he discusses insights linking the development of our grasping reflex coincided with the development of our tongue and vocal cords. It seems that tool manipulation and communication co-exist in adaptive responses. So significant is the role of the hands in problem solving that organisations such as NASA and IMB will not take people who don't have a history of tinkering. They have found non-tinkerers just don't have the same kind of problem solving skills. Object manipulation and knowing the world with your hands strengthens confidence and psychological connection with the world. By handling objects we pair up visual information and this plays a critical role in creating visuospatial images.

There are many practices that involve making together and these often involve repetitive actions that free up space for open and trusting emergent communication. Think of painting, sanding, stitching, weaving. Many indigenous cultures have active practices that hold space for making, talking and connecting. Art therapy practices are also tapping into these insights to rebuild connections communally and individually. When you are involved in a making activity, notice the kind of conversation that arises. Cooking and gardening are good examples.

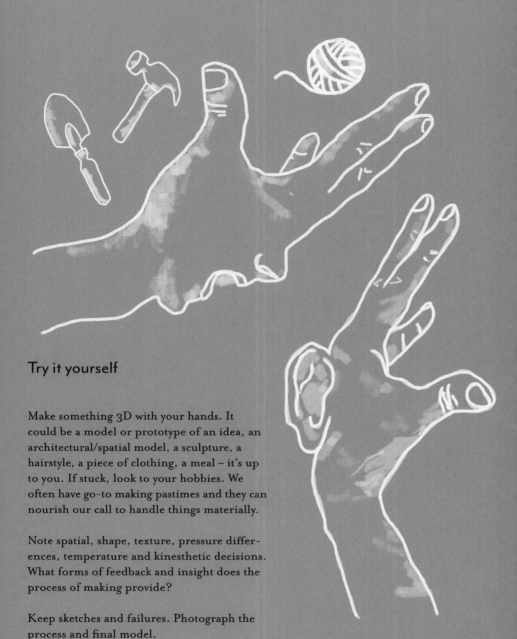

Try it yourself

Make something 3D with your hands. It could be a model or prototype of an idea, an architectural/spatial model, a sculpture, a hairstyle, a piece of clothing, a meal – it's up to you. If stuck, look to your hobbies. We often have go-to making pastimes and they can nourish our call to handle things materially.

Note spatial, shape, texture, pressure differences, temperature and kinesthetic decisions. What forms of feedback and insight does the process of making provide?

Keep sketches and failures. Photograph the process and final model.

Background

Audio description is the art of communicating when vision isn't accessible. It's a form of narration that consists of information about key elements, qualities and movements. It helps us to explain visuals so others can understand what they are about and/or access to shared realms.

When using audio describing, it is important to not only describe what is happening in the visual but to talk about the feelings, emotions or atmosphere that it provokes as well. Audio describing also affords a widening out of our awareness and brings attention to the intersections of sensory information that shapes experiences we call visual. Many creative practices draw on the senses and often-times a work that becomes realised visually, begins its life as multi sensory encounters. By seeking out the range of sensations that shape visual experience we find ourselves in a shared continuum that diversifies how we perceive and commune.

'The Oregon Project' is an interactive audio visual experience created by Keith Salmon and Neel Joshi in collaboration with Microsoft. They focus the project around the question, 'How does one enjoy and consume visual artworks if they have visual impairment'.

The room is full of bright, warm sunshine. The door is open and there's a feeling of a gentle breeze. Yellow sunflowers in the garden give a happy feeling. The floor is clean, the room neat with slippers carefully arranged outside.

Try it yourself

Choose a section of a movie you really love or find evocative (2-3 mins will be ample). Create an audio recording of the scene for someone who is vision impaired.

Consider the following focus areas within the scene:
- Feeling
- Mood, facial expressions
- Atmosphere
- Key details
- Focus points
- Movements and directions in the space
- Pace
- Design elements such as furnishings (soft and hard) and clothing (including textural properties)
- Cultural context (e.g messages, symbols and intended audiences)

Background

Alternative text, commonly known as 'alt text', are text labels attached to images on web pages. Alt text is read by screen reader software to explain the image content to people who are visually impaired or may not otherwise be able to access the images. Alt text is also used by search engines to help rank pages based on how relevant their content is to the searcher. Good alt text is concise and specific, sharing the most important information about an image for the intended audience.

The approaches for alt text have also been explored by artists – Bojana Coklyat and Shannon Finnegan worked with Eyebeam and the Disability Visibility Project in the United States to produce 'Alt Text As Poetry', a creative workbook for those learning about alt text. For inspiration on how to approach alt text, Coklyat and Finnegan look to poetry: a form where economic word use, close attention to language, and an experimental ethos are all key creative components. In their resource they also provide several exercises, which we have drawn inspiration from in developing this creative method.

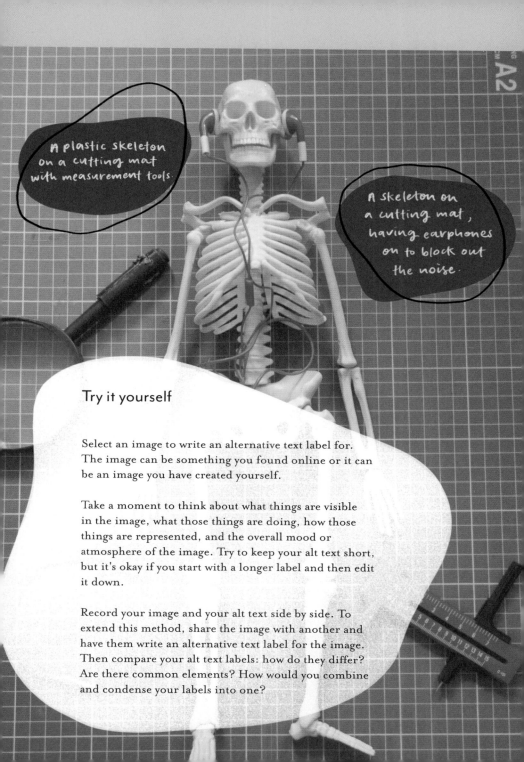

Try it yourself

Select an image to write an alternative text label for. The image can be something you found online or it can be an image you have created yourself.

Take a moment to think about what things are visible in the image, what those things are doing, how those things are represented, and the overall mood or atmosphere of the image. Try to keep your alt text short, but it's okay if you start with a longer label and then edit it down.

Record your image and your alt text side by side. To extend this method, share the image with another and have them write an alternative text label for the image. Then compare your alt text labels: how do they differ? Are there common elements? How would you combine and condense your labels into one?

Background

Most of us are embedded in a variety of communities. Reliable and diverse communities support our wellbeing and enrich us culturally and creatively. They also form the ecosystems that support us directly and indirectly. They are part of our working lives, be it through private or public organisations, our domestic and personal lives, the infrastructures that make connection possible and of course the natural systems that foster existence itself.

Giving space for diverse lives (human and non-human) and their unique niche in the world can help us see anew – it is creative fodder. While our world has become increasingly networked, often with remote and quite virtual kinds of connections, research from Robin Dunbar at the University of Liverpool indicates that the average person retains a meaningful network of about 150 people.

One way to enrich our lives and the way we connect is to engage in a deep conversation with people we might not otherwise. Conversation is a kind of mind reading game where we are guessing what others are thinking and why they say it.

Theodore Zeldin has championed the value of conversations and his 'conversation dinners' have become renowned. In these dinners, strangers are given a menu of conversation topics to stimulate thought-provoking discussion.

Try it yourself

Part 1: Mapping conversation networks

Map out people who are meaningful in your networks. Even if you don't interact often, look to register diversity such as:
- Elders or members of an older generation
- Children
- Local community people: garbage collectors, council workers, superiors, juniors, hairdressers, colleagues or co-workers, or those at the local supermarket or garage
- People who are involved in supporting your working and domestic life (e.g. cleaners, administrators, community small business owners)
- Natural life - animals, plants/living systems

Giving each a code (e.g. colour or symbol) will make the map easier to read.

Part 2: The conversation cafe

Pick 5 people in your network including 2 people that are more formally linked. With each, initiate a conversation that takes you into new territory (i.e. things you wouldn't usually discuss).

Helpful tips: give it space and time, use a ritual like a walk or visiting a cafe.

Note down new perspectives, surprises or learnings from the conversation.

If you are stuck – here are some conversation starters:
- When is silence a virtue
- How much money do people need to earn
- Beauty and buildings
- Food is for...
- Being on time
- Laziness can be good when...

Lee Cooper – Vitality, small talk and social space.

Lee is an experienced leader within the not-for-profit and charity sector, with a focus on organizational improvement across drug and alcohol and homelessness services. Lee has noticed a trend across a number of organizations, where process is put ahead of people.

"When things go wrong, there is an assumption that it is because people didn't follow the agreed process. The response is then to improve the process and communicate the change.

The problem with this response is that it treats a complex situation as if there is a known solution, and it doesn't give the people working within the situation the authority to draw on their experience to respond to the situation in front of them. This removes essential elements that create vitality in the system.

Lee is developing practical tools to create space for conversations and the generation of a vitality narrative within the sector. Vitality has emerged within our community of practice as an aspirational concept that goes beyond other aspirational values such as resilience, or sustainability. Vitality speaks to an energy and ability to live, grow, and develop.

"No change is possible without a shared understanding and shared story for the future we hope to inspire. Through introducing storytelling we can create that new narrative that includes drawing on the experience of people in the sector."

Lee developed four activities all aimed at being done within a group setting to spark conversations about vitality, two of them are featured here.

Small Talk – People from across different communities provide daily postcards for seven days around topics of shared value. The postcards are then read in a collaborative workshop with the emerging themes informing the path to action.

Social Spaces – Engage local partners, create a photo collage of spaces and places around the local area.
Participants then walk around locations taking photos of places that inspire hope, feel safe, feel unsafe, create a sense of hopelessness, need to be fixed, are unique, makes them feel proud or ashamed.
Sort the photos into themes and explore the stories behind the them. What are the narratives? How do the spaces change over time?

"My reason for choosing the activities is based on two criteria. Primarily I was looking for activities that had a readiness for creativity. I want to draw out the creativity that exists within people in the organizations I work with, but also create a balance. Going too far too soon may have negative results like not being seen as legitimate 'business' activity. Secondly, I want to push myself within this work as well as balance the need to get the best outcome for the organisations I work with."

These activities are then used as input into a typical strategic planning process.

"Importantly the creative elements don't take away from strategic planning, they are not a 'nice to do' or 'warm and fuzzy warm up activity' but important part of creating an innovative ecosystem."

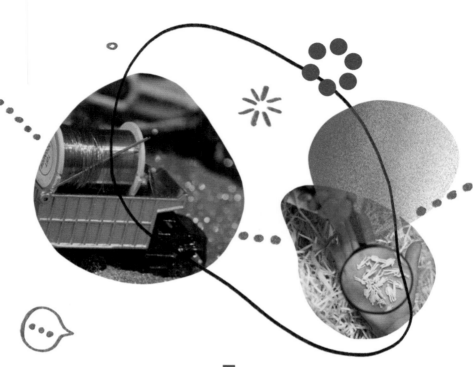

stories

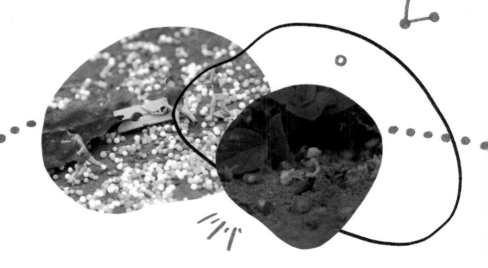

Stories are one of the most remarkable aptitudes humans have in their creative suite. They make our shifting lives intelligible. They are adaptable, colourful, tap into our memories and synthesise the emotional soup of our lives – warts and all. They thread together visions of the past, present and future. They help us to reconcile inconsistencies, tensions, empathise, imagine and make messiness navigable.

Psychological studies have shown how the stories we tell sculpt what we see and value and thus, bring into existence. Stories are powerful, playful and persistent. We use myths and fables to process long arcs of time and to reproduce social and cultural norms (with tweaks). Sometimes we do this explicitly and other times it can be more covert – a self revealing story can reclothe and recast older patterns.

Stories are mobilised by a spectrum of creative methods and practices. They also summon the embodied and sensorial memories that we give metaphoric form. Stories are embellished with symbols and conveyed through the many mediums we use to communicate. We find our narratives through filtering and playing with frames, crossing boundaries, overlaying and trans-muting ways of knowing. Stories help us converge our experiences and recalibrate - they are a great way to bring our imaginative work to the ground and generate space for collectively making sense of the what, why, how and where to next.

Background

Stories are mobilised through characters. They might not be human, but making them human-like helps us switch on our mirror neurons and empathy pathways. This is one way we can find ourselves in the lives of others, allowing us to travel time and space by suspending our disbelief. But, in order to do so we need to feel characters are relatable.

Animators, theatre and film makers, game builders, and increasingly the full spectrum of design practices, all work with character creation. For director Julie Taymor, a key part of any dramatic process is to find the 'ideograph of a moment', the scene where a character is reduced to its essence 'like a Japanese brush painting'. Animation studio Pixar are renowned for innovating in graphics technology, often spending months of research and development to accurately render character details like the folds of clothes and hair, or the way gestures convey a character's personality.

Try it yourself

Create a character based on a personality or occupational role you would like or dislike in your world. You could do this on paper, digitally or bring to life with your body by dressing up.

1. **Build a character and give them:**
   - A name (try baby name sites for inspiration)
   - A history and family life
   - Some individual quirks e.g. loveable to some more annoying to others, 'details' oriented, a social connector
   - A rebellious tweak and a more traditional or conservative trait
   - Dress your character. Think about these elements: colour, style, influences, context/situation, group membership

ACDC

Loves
ACDC

Designer

Allergic
to Lavender

Has
Lisp

2. **Give your character nuance and surprise:**
· Give them an allergy
· A super power
· Switch clothing or music preferences for one
· Find their musical taste/s
· Do they have pets
· What are their habits and hobbies/ pastimes
· Give them a smell or give their house a smell
· A physical skill or hobby
· An accent or style of talking
· An animal characteristic or two, e.g wise like an owl or
  playful like a puppy

Nervous
around
Birds

Background

Scenography involves the union of practices that build worlds and create environments in which 'performance' takes place. It is a broad umbrella that spans theatre, film, TV and all kinds of events (music, catwalks, conferences, seminars, dinners and costume). This field also reaches into architectural and spatial design including offices, museums and visual merchandising. Embedded in this realm are the elements that establish the atmosphere and timbre of a staging including light, sound, structure, spatial use, decorative embellishment and clothing.

Scenography is the art of heightening and intensifying experiences in space. German philosopher Gernot Böhme has unpacked the dynamics of 'felt' spaces and the 'atmospheres' they shape. He draws attention to a range of subtle interactions such as material qualities, surface texture, light colour and acoustics. Over time this has expanded the range of qualities that scenographers include in their design palette which increasingly draws on multi-sensory and immaterial or ephemeral elements such as kinaesthetic interactions, scent and taste. As notions of performance space expand and interests in immersive and interactive experiences grow, interest in scenography grows.

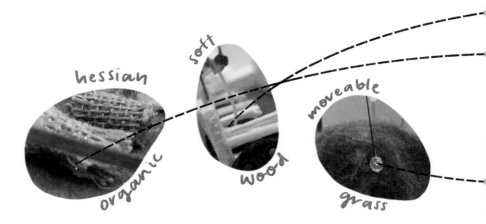

Try it yourself

Create a (physical or digital) mood board or maquette (scale model) encapsulating a particular atmosphere or felt experiences. You are looking to evoke a range of references or the 'vibe' with either samples or a mock up that may draw on:

- Light
- Colour palette of the room, objects, costumes
- Textures and materials for surfaces and objects
- Sound
- Stylistic influences, eras, design or artistic influences
- Cultural or mythical archetypes
- Pattern
- Iconic references e.g. architecture, fashion, movie stills, photography, video clips, poems, paintings or images

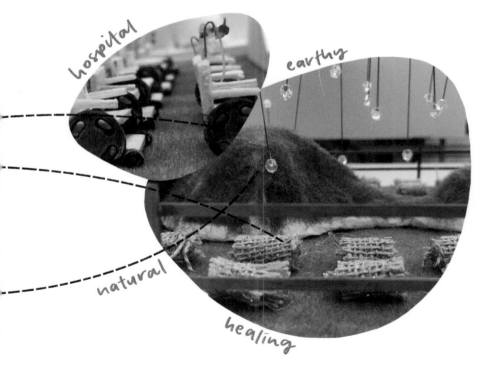

hospital

earthy

natural

healing

Background

"Words mean more than what is set down on paper. It takes the human voice to infuse them with deeper meaning." - Maya Angelou.

There is a saying that your voice is the instrument of your being. Actors, singers and presenters know this and spend time experimenting with their vocal range and resonance while honing the use of their bodies. As air waves marry with complex biochemical pulsations and anatomical form, emotion and meaning take on new life.

Our voices form experiences of unity and spatial interaction. They can be used well, be pushed into states of stress and transmit subtle, embodied cues. The tone and quality of our voice can capture attention, lull and conversely, repel.

We also gesture with intonation, emphasis and word choices. The way we vocalise shapes context and sense, making atmosphere. Our use of profanity is one example as cognitive scientist Ben Bergen has unpacked in his research. Expletives might use taboo words, but the shape we give to them can be wide ranging from excitement and surprise to frustration and despair.

Voices are vehicles of storytelling, yet we don't often pay much attention to the act of voicing. This exercise taps into some of the methods actors, singers, presenters, politicians, health practitioners and dramaturgs use to hone the use and awareness of this organic instrument as a vital conveyer of story.

As you go about your day, listen to people talking - notice how they are using their voice and how interactions between situational factors and moods can be influential.

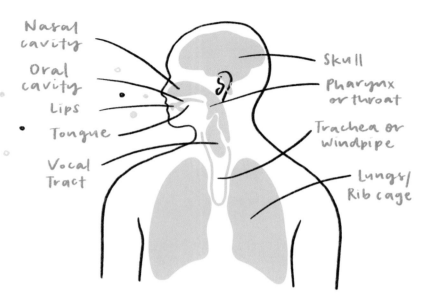

Nasal cavity

Oral cavity

Lips

Tongue

Vocal Tract

Skull

Pharynx or throat

Trachea or windpipe

Lungs/ Rib cage

Try it yourself

To warm up for this exercise, first listen to people talking, voicing and expressing. Observe how voices connect/disconnect with other bodies or bounce off surfaces.

Create a sketch of an outline of the human body to record your experiments below:

- Block your ears and close your eyes. Make sounds with vowels, then make words and notice how consonants create closure around vowels. Words as simple as yes and no provide a good range.
- Feel your voice vibrating and resonating inside your body. Track how and where the sounds move.
- Experiment by making sounds and opening your mouth, not moving your tongue, smiling and squishing up your nose.
- Stretch your tongue – try to get a few yawns in then stick your tongue out as far as you can, reach for your chin, touch your nose. Notice where there is tension.

Background

Rituals are behavioural anchors that help orient experiences in time and space. Shared by many species, they are performed to nourish a sense of connection that includes daily individual and group routines through to mass gatherings that inject the air with heightened energies and elaborate ceremonies. Anthropologist Clifford Geertz says rituals fulfil a special role for people in that they help build a bridge between a life that could be experienced as endless, disorienting chaos by creating form and structure that create an aura of order.

Rituals are clothed in symbols and signs that are multi directional: they point to where we have come from and suggest how we might shape the way forward. These signalling systems are adaptive, multisensory performances. Neuroscientists such as Antonio Damasio and Iain McGilchrist have extended these ideas by pointing to the adaptive role stories play in collective sense making which can help modulate stress responses – a kind of dance that seeks out balance between stimulation, stress and under activity. Rituals sit in the space in-between, on the one hand creating stabilising habits and on the other the possibility of heightened experience.

Rituals have tended to be seen in a more traditional light, especially with historical influences of societies, religions and cultures. We have a myriad of rituals in today's world, including new online and offline rituals. Our experiences adapt to time and process and inversely, ritual and habits transmute shape us. Rituals are often mobilised by symbols, signs and incantations. Anthropologist Carole Counihan has long studied the links between food, culture and ritual. Her examination of fast food chains, uniforms and incantations 'would you like fries with that' shows how rituals morph between ideologies and contexts.

Try it yourself

Create a set of rituals for a character or persona. This can be the first that comes to mind, it doesn't need much detail or thought for this part. Then step into their world and embellish it with rituals.

Create three rituals to get them through the day. Note any symbols or signs that are involved. These rituals could be:
- A seasonal ritual
- An annual ritual
- A ritual for the morning, daytime and the night
- A ritual that maintains tradition
- An esoteric ritual
- A ritual for crises
- A ritual for an unknown future
- A ritual of your own distinct creation

Animate

Background

Most of us will have encountered stories where the characters are non-human or have been given anthropomorphic qualities. When we animate, we take qualities that are frozen in time and through motion imbue a range of living traits. By breathing life into the equation we introduce purpose and social or nonsocial responses that shape seen and unforeseen changes. We can play with collaboration, interactive impacts, memory and lines of reasoning. Patterns and interactions can reveal organising principles such as scale and language (including made up intonation and gestures).

Animating can also expose subtle preferences in attention such as picking up looped sequences in microseconds, evaluative scans for living vs mechanical reproduction. An organic or mild asymmetry seems more organic and living than perfect symmetry. Keep an eye out for animated depictions of living and non living/machine systems – what do you notice?

Pioneer animator Jan Svankmajer says "For me, animated film is about magic. This is how magic becomes part of daily life, invading daily life…. Magic enters into a quite ordinary contact with mundane things".

Try it yourself

Turn two objects you use frequently into characters and create a conversation between them. They might tell each other what their day to day lives are like, or you could include a challenge or gripe.

There are a range of ways to animate:
- A voice or video recording
- A comic strip
- Stop motion
- Dramatised dialogue
- Photo burst, slow motion or time-lapse on your phone camera

To extend this, you could give your characters two occupations, or distinct animal or plant personas. Cause them to meet en route somewhere – what advice can they offer each other based on their unique experience of life?

Background

Mnemonic systems embedded into time and place-based stories build memory palaces which live inside our own bodies as much as the outside world. They are techniques for focusing our attention towards the systems we depend on – the weather, ecologies, land-scapes, families, trade and sacred (or protected) understandings held by elders or masters of a realm.

Indigenous cultures demonstrate how memorised information is linked to surviving and thriving. Information is retained and passed on through stories, pictures, songs and dances that are integrated with space, place and time. These traditions are not only detailed and complex, but they can survive accurately for tens of thousands of years. This kind of knowledge spans all sorts of interactions, from seemingly incidental conversations to cyclical passages marking time. In western systems these might be recognised via the clock, calendar, seasons, regular events and ceremonial occasions.

Method of loci

The method of loci technique can be linked to building a kind of memory palace. It involves chunking information into small parts, connecting each chunk with a unique signifier (an image or sensory trigger e.g. building, sound, movement or scent) and then mentally placing these signifiers on a 'path' in an environ-ment you know well – e.g. your house, your neighbourhood or your workplace. Once established, the signifier can be added to. The aim is to build your knowledge by recalling and recounting preferably through sound and movement.

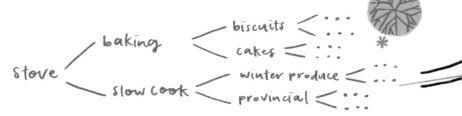

stove — baking — biscuits < . . .
            cakes < . . .
      — slow cook — winter produce < . . .
            provincial < . . .

Try it yourself

Build (or extend) a memory palace that consciously aims to amplify how you engage space and others. Consider these elements:

1. Scan your environment for memories and associations. Is there a wall, image, plant, scent, seat or other object that stimulates a memory?
2. Can you take these connections and add extra information or them give another flavour?
3. Consider new practices or details you would like to build into your environment. Look for spatial, visual and temporal cues to extra associations.
4. Create simple, repeatable and connecting triggers to help you hold new information and keep adding to it. Over time you will develop increasingly complex connections linking place and space to the details of life and cycles of time.

Create a visual representation of your space – this could be a simple sketch map or set of 360 photographs. Mark out key locations and when you add details tell the story aloud. Over time look to remove the map and test your memory by using place-based cues to verbally recall the detail.

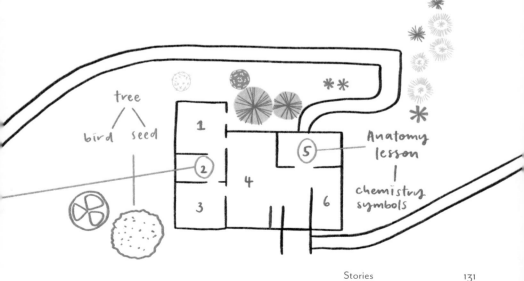

Background

Stories are unifiers of the arts and our creative capacities. Stories help us find ways to make our wisdom understandable, transmissible, persuasive and emotionally moving.

Neuroscientists such as Iain McGilchrist and Antonio Damasio agree that storytelling is something our minds do in creating and changing ourselves. The art and practice of story pervades the entire fabric of human societies and cultures. Damasio suggests that stories play a biological role "as a homeostatic device for artist and recipient and as a means of communication". This kind of idea has found traction in magnetic resonance imaging (MRI) that shows neural coupling. When the brain hears or sees a story, mirror neurons fire in the same patterns as the storyteller's brain.

Stories help us to navigate our way through experiences woven with paradox, chaos and cycles of change. So significant is the role of storytelling that Damasio regards story masters like Shakespeare as special kinds of muse neuroscientists.

How to approach stories

The art and value of story has also been explored extensively by Joseph Campbell who uses the hero's journey as a narrative framework.

Though there are many ways to tell stories, we have become comfortable with the linear Three Act structure: the Setup, the Confrontation and the Resolution.

In recent times, non-linear and divergent story telling has gained traction particularly through gaming and interactive technologies. It can be useful to notice the differences between linear and non-linear storylines.

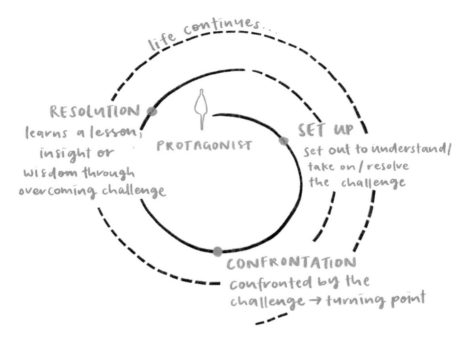

life continues...

RESOLUTION
learns a lesson,
insight or
wisdom through
overcoming challenge

PROTAGONIST

SET UP
set out to understand/
take on / resolve
the challenge

CONFRONTATION
confronted by the
challenge → turning point

Try it yourself

Make a short story that communicates a tension, surprise and creative hope. Aim to impart your message story within 5 minutes or less.

There's lots of options in how you convey your story such as:
- A short script for film, TV or theatre (here movement, action and props are also important)
- A poem, song/ballad or segment of a saga
- A cartoon or zine
- An aural account (recorded)
- A sequence of music
- A children's picture book
- A game

Background

Collages are a kind of rich picture on steroids. They can generate complex and varied meanings through layerings of scale, juxtaposing symbols, uses of multiple media such as fragments of text and pattern. Collages can evoke dream like worlds and draw people into conversation.

Diverse narratives

A detailed collage can act as rich dialogue space where people bring their own sense making histories into a kind of non-linear exchange. What emerges is a place for swirling stories. Some intersect and others might collide, repel or drift to edges. The offer in this context is to listen deeply, to suspend judgement and witness diversity in the ways people make sense. Psychologists, artists, health workers and social researchers use these kinds of approaches to open up dialogue while honouring that we are all storytellers. This approach has been widely used in psychology and art from Dadaists to Surrealists and in Jungian Sandplay therapy. Collages can open pathways for non verbal memory and inarticulable experience. Sociologist Arthur Frank in his seminal work 'The Wounded Storyteller' says that space for diverse narratives is vital for collective well being. In this kind of storytelling space, the endings are provisional and leave openings for more stories.

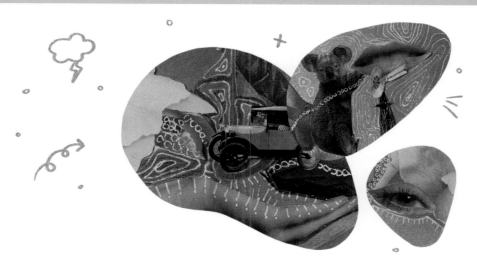

Try it yourself

Create a collage. It can be 2D cut out images, a 3D assemblage of small objects or a set of phrases or story snippets. The elements can be fixed (pasted) into position or remain moveable for multiple arrangements. They can also be analogue or digital.

Ask others to join you in building, morphing and making sense of the collage. Listen and ask questions to clarify or extend the stories.

Consider these prompts for discussion:
- Are there underlying themes and what might drive them into the open?
- Do stories reference difficult conditions or hold resources for coping?
- Is there potential for stories to be dangerous or perhaps deprecating to others?
- Who is brought together and who might be left outside?
- How might other stories connect up or run alongside others?
- How might stories help us to explore and discover new possibilities?

Case study

Christina Luzi — A new festival frame.

Christina is a leader at a high-school that is actively exploring and shaping their relationship with the surrounding community. Taking on this challenge during a global pandemic adds another complexity.

"The COVID 19 virus has impacted many facets of life. In schools it has significantly impacted the relationship and partnership between parents and caregivers and the community.

As much as we have become comfortable ordering clothing and other consumables online without having seen them in person first, COVID 19 forces families to "order their school" online. As families were not permitted on school sites throughout 2020, many families were forced to select their child's High schools without ever having set foot on the school site.

As schools were permitted to open their doors (in some capacity) in June of 2021, there was an increasing pressure on schools to ensure that their communities felt welcome to step foot through the College doors and tour where their child would finish their formal education. In a school community of over 2000, this meant significant pressure to deliver."

Having adapted to remote learning the open day was a significant opportunity to take the initiative within a fluid environment. Rather than reverting to the way open days had run in the past, Christina gathered her colleagues and ran them through a collaborative framing exercise.

"A group of educators, parents and students came together, we asked ourselves "why". Why the school tour? What did it mean for parents, students and teachers?

As we began to unpack this "why" our discussion kept leading us back to "authentic partnership" between the parents, students and the school. We wanted to create a space where conversations and rituals come together as we made new memories together. So we decided to make this feel like a "festival" where all we had to offer our students was showcased.

We set a challenge to the students and teachers, asking them to "showcase their spaces" and create the opportunity for the attendees to "put in" and "take from" their spaces."

In setting this challenge, Christina and the organisers of the open day gave the whole school the opportunity to create a festival that celebrated the school community.

"The result of this was phenomenal, we saw immersive experiences for the guests where they were able to hear from current students, they were able to participate in experiments, observe students recording a live podcast, and see our technology spaces in action.

We also had two live stages with our college bands and ensembles performing, our entertainment students running the sound and lighting. Our hospitality students cooked, catered over 2000 sweet and savory food items. We wanted to make this feel like a "festival" where all we had to offer our students was showcased.

We focused on not doing it how we had always done and focused on ensuring that every "stage" showcased our amazing learning community, that it challenged the families to be involved and high-lighted that our community of learners was gaining new members."

By creating the space for her colleagues to creatively explore this new festival frame, Christina gave them the ownership of the event, and brought in a vitality that energised the relationship between the school and the community.

Simon Byrne – People, energy and land.

Simon trained and practiced in law, he moved into strategic planning and works as a member of the executive leadership group of a large shipping port. The port has been a central element of the community for many thousands of years. The Awabakal clan of the Muloobina nation are the traditional custodians of the land and the water. Upon colonisation the ancient middens were burnt to create lime for construction and the area was renamed Newcastle.

In recent history, the port has exported energy. Energy that has been embodied in steel that has built cities and structures around the world. Presently the port exports energy in the form of high-quality coal that is used to make steel and create electricity. With such a proud and long history, the port city is, as always, adapting to and shaping the future.

"In the last 30-50 years Newcastle has been seen as an industrial city. Working class, hardworking, and built on coal and steel. But as a port, it has always been about much more than what we load on the ships."

There have been many voices seeking to shape the future of Newcastle from outside; Newcastle as a 'smart city', etc. Simon is looking to the future by connecting with the inner Newcastle.

"Having arrived here only a couple of years ago, I've been wondering how to connect with the local people broadly, and the innovators. I've tried a few things and all of the way have had my eyes and mind open to the possibilities. There is a real pride to this community, it is a great strength."

Simon drew from his new kit-bag of creative methods and supported by his Masters program colleagues convened people from his emerging innovation ecosystem.

"We came together every Thursday evening for six weeks, interviewing people from my fledgling network, taking insights from those interviews into a workshop with the network and creating a small buzz and a feeling of vitality amongst my network."

Simon had developed a suite of creative methods that he was using with his network to explore the future of Newcastle, and its past. In order to move into the future, Simon was seeking an understanding of the heart and soul of Newcastle.

Over six weeks the team with Simon used an array of creative practices and methods:
· Renku; Japanese inspired, collaborative linked verse poetry
· Probing interviews followed by grounded theory analysis to identify themes
· Theme exploration that went deep into the underlying meaning created through the interviews
· Pecha Kucha presentations on the themes
· Collaborative workshops creating memes, possible futures, and energising the emerging innovation ecosystem

"There is an energy to Newcastle. The energy comes from the land and is carried by the people. The people of Newcastle have helped build the world that we know. They will be there building the future as well."

Contributors to this book:

The seeds for this book have been born of a creative root system where creative methods and practices have been formed, reformed and passed on over time. Creativity finds meeting places to enrich and amplify its pulse. In conceiving this book, the TD School at UTS (Transdisciplinary School, University of Technology Sydney) is one such incubator and catalyser. Here, scholars, students, industry practitioners and diverse communities have shared a rich array of creative approaches that have won global awards for transformational teaching and learning and pollinated the exercises within this book. In turn, they are offered to you to transmute and transmit so we can collectively thrive.

This book also forms part of a growing compendium of linked publications including 'Designing for the common good' and 'Frame Innovation: Create new thinking by design'. To find out more about these and forthcoming publications see **https://www.cisix.org**

Authors
Barbara Doran

Barbara is a scholar and practitioner in creativity. She specialises in identifying creative opportunities that respond to complex challenges and putting them in action. Her skills are drawn from working across the arts, the tertiary sector and from project experience in the private, public and community sectors which bring together practical, imaginative, playful and collaborative outcomes. She is a multi-awarded artist and her experience spans working across the realms of collective well-being including public health, urban and regional planning, health psychology and the arts. It is this range of experience that has informed a transdisciplinary layering of how to engage and ignite creative intelligence in practical and inspiring ways. Barbara is based in the TD School, UTS University of Technology, Sydney.

Rodger Watson

Rodger is an innovator for public good and has worked as a public servant, strategic human centred design consultant, bartender, pizza deliverer, emu farmhand, and the leader of an academic research centre. He is founding Course Director of the Master of Creative Intelligence and Strategic Innovation at TD School, University of Technology Sydney. With his colleagues at the Designing Out Crime Research Centre, he pioneered the Designing for the Common Good approach to multi-stakeholder collaboration. This was recognised by the Australian Research Council as highly impactful in the 2018-19 Research Impact Assessment. In recent years Rodger has contributed to government strategy across topics ranging from domestic and family violence, mental health, built environment, counter terrorism, night-time economy, waste & circular economy, environmental protection, cybercrime, and transport innovation.

Diana Vo

Diana Vo is a Sydney-based creative designer, curious thinker, and storyteller at heart. She is passionate about how design and visual communication has the power to make complex problems accessible for any audience and build better futures. She thrives on the opportunity to address and confront pressing issues in our world by leaning into design as a space to help others to think, ponder and question. She has an unwavering belief that creativity is found in all places and that design communication opens up new ways of discovering endless possibilities. Diana is a Visual Communication (Honours) graduate from the University of Technology Sydney and works with the TD School.

Nina Pirola

Is a visual communications designer who works at the intersection of problem solving and effective design. She specialises in trans-disciplinary thinking and human centred design in making changes guided by empathy and positive social and environmental impact.

Rory Green

Rory Green is a writer, editor and learning designer living on Gadigal land in Sydney, Australia. Rory works with the TD School UTS and has been involved in the design and delivery of several innovative subjects including the subjects that sit alongside this book.

Justine Hauser

Justine has served in the defence force for more than 25 years. In this time she has had many roles and has worked in a huge variety of situations. As a professional Justine has become adept at navigating rigid situations, where hierarchy and procedure are key. Justine makes space for the humanity of the situation to emerge, bringing out the best in the people around her. Justine is Masters candidate in the UTS Master of Creative Intelligence and Strategic Innovation.

Andrew Trieu

Andrew Trieu is an innovative Change Manager who works across a range of contexts within the private, public, and not-for-profit sectors. He is President of AIESEC Alumni Australia and is an alumni of the UTS Graduate Certificate of Public Sector Innovation, and a contributor to the Master of Creative Intelligence and Strategic Innovation community at TD School, UTS.

Lee Wallace

Lee Wallace is a social innovator with a history in public policy in Environment and legislative review. Lee challenges the status quo with a productive mindset, fuelled by a curious spirit. Lee is a pioneering alum of the UTS Graduate Certificate of Public Sector Innovation and an active contributor to the Master of Creative Intelligence and Strategic innovation at UTS.

Carl Heise

Carl Heise is the leader of a business architecture team within a very large transport agency. From his background as a high-school drama teacher Carl brings a playful curiosity to organisational challenges. Carl is a contributor to the Master of Creative Intelligence and Strategic Innovation community at TD School, UTS.

Lee Cooper

Lee Cooper is an executive-level leader within the not-for-profit and charity sector. Lee is focused on a future that moves beyond a procedural paradigm and adopts a consultative & collaborative approach to lead teams to get the best ideas out of people to make the biggest impact. In this mix, Lee is intentionally curious and values hands-on experience. Lee is a contributor to the Master of Creative Intelligence and Strategic Innovation community at TD School, UTS.

Christina Luzi

Christina Luzi is Director of Teaching and Learning at an innovative 21st Century K-12 Learning Community. Christina is a passionate educator and custodian of the future leaders of our world. She is a dynamic contributor to the Masters of Creative Intelligence and Strategic Innovation community at TD School, UTS and is actively involved in a growing network of people driving change in their organisations.

Simon Byrne

Simon Byrnes trained and practiced in commercial law. He now works as a chief commercial officer at a global port. He has worked across many sectors including rail, road, airports and ports. Simon is one of the founding contributors to the UTS Master of Creative Intelligence and Strategic Innovation.